QUANTUM ACTIVATION CARDS

Companion Gui•ebook

KAREN CURRY PARKER

For permissions contact:

HUMAN
DESIGN
P R E S S

An Imprint for GracePoint Matrix Publishing (www.GracePointPublishing.com),
a Division of GracePoint Matrix, LLC

PUBLISHING

322 N Tejon St. #207
Colorado Springs CO 80903

www.GracePointMatrix.com

Email: Admin@GracePointMatrix.com

SAN # 991-6032

For bulk order requests and price schedule please email:
Orders@GracePointPublishing.com

Contents

Welcome

You are a once-in-a-lifetime cosmic event!

You were born at this time for a very specific reason—you are here to usher in a new Creative Era that promises to help create a sustainable, equitable and peaceful world.

This purpose you are called to serve isn't about what you do, your work or your career. You serve this purpose by being the full expression of who you are. You, being the person you were born to be, is the most vital contribution you can make to the world.

When you are living true to yourself, in authentic alignment with your True Identity and expressing who you are without compromise, you become sustainable. You use your energy to create more of what you want with minimal resistance and avoidance.

You are a dreamer, a cosmic revolutionary. There is much you have forgotten. It's time to remember Who You Truly Are, defined by your innate creative power and how to take your vital, unique and irreplaceable part in the Cosmic Plan.

As we stand on the brink of a powerful collective shift in consciousness, the world needs you to fulfill your destiny. The more you align with the true story of who you are and craft a personal narrative that is worthy of who you are, the more you add to the energy and the experience of well-being to the world.

It is time for you to take your place as a leader in this New World.

As a Leader, you have to consciously and deliberately craft a consistent faith-based energy that calls into your life the support you need to stretch yourself beyond what you can simply create on your own. You need to trust the Universe—unwaveringly, be willing to take risks and get uncomfortable as you grow and serve an evolving world.

But, you can only lift the vibration of others to the level of your own vibration. The more you live in alignment with your Authentic Self, the higher the frequency of your energy. The higher you take your own frequency of energy, the more you create the energy for others to rise with you.

This truly is the fulfillment of your purpose. Being yourself is the most precious work you can do on the planet at this time. May the information on these cards, serve you in aligning more deeply with the true story of who you are.

A Message from the Author

Many years ago, I wrote that we need to stop healing and start "whole-in". We need to stop buying into the idea that we are broken, stuck or blocked. We need to start living from that unlimited, whole, creative place of our own potential inside each of us that can be released when we let go of the old stories that no longer serve us.

You're not broken, stuck or blocked. All of the factors necessary for you to lead an abundant and powerful life are contained within you.

Letting go of old stories and rewriting a personal narrative is not always an easy thing to do.

We are conditioned by many factors that influence our perception of Self. Sorting through the myriad of experiences and other factors that create an individuals story can be daunting and overwhelming.

Quantum Human Design gets to the root cause of why we do the things we do and why we make the creative choices that we make. It gives us a system to bypass our conditioning and rewrite our personal narrative so that we can start "whole-in" and tapping into a new empowered story that is befitting of the true being of who we are.

The brain is hard-wired to be on the alert for disaster and tragedy, making us biologically inclined to expect the worst and to be prepared for everything to go wrong. In some ways this has worked because this kind of primal thinking has the capacity to keep us alive under extreme circumstances.

Not only are our brains hard-wired to be on the defensive, but also our life experiences have conditioned us and have limited the options we think are possible for us to create. The way your family of origin behaved and what they believed coupled with your own life experiences and even your genetic predisposition "set you up" for certain patterns and expectations. These past events may be limiting what you're allowing yourself to believe you can experience in your own life.

Scientists now know some of the choices people make with their lives are conditioned by ancestral memory (known as epigenetics) that influence how your DNA and cells function. Epigenes can also influence reaction to the conditions in life.

You can be influenced by up to 14 generations of ancestral memories in your cells. This means that some of your choices and reactions are being influenced by things that happened hundreds of years before you were even born and are a compilation of the experiences of over 65,000 grandparents in your bloodline.

In addition to your unique epigenetics, you are also energetically conditioned. Anything on your Human Design chart that is "white" or "undefined" shows where you absorb and amplify energy from the world around you. Your chart's "undefined" energy is where you are designed to experience the world and to become wise about others through this experience.

It's pretty easy to take in energy in your "undefined" parts of your chart and mistakenly identify with it; this causes you to allow your own energy to be "hijacked". In these "open" energies, you can think you are someone you are not and thus you adopt predictable behavioral patterns that may help you cope with the intensity of how you experience these energies.

You are designed to use your experience in your "undefined" elements of your chart to choose how you want to express these energies in the world. Where you are "open" in your chart gives you choices and freedom to express these energies in the way you want. However, you have to master the ebb and flow of this energy as you move through the world.

The parts of your chart that are colored, called "defined" in Human Design, are also influencing the choices you make and how you create. The "definition" in your chart indicates key personality traits and energies from which you learn as well as on which you will expand over the course of your life.

THE HUMAN DESIGN BODYGRAPH

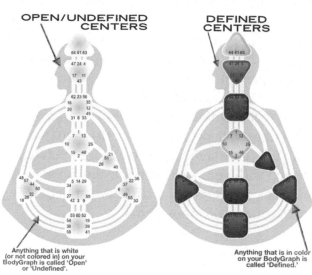

OPEN/UNDEFINED CENTERS

DEFINED CENTERS

Anything that is white (or not colored in) on your BodyGraph is called 'Open' or 'Undefined'.

Anything that is in color on your BodyGraph is called 'Defined.'

Your beliefs, life experiences and past learning all influence how you express and perceive yourself. Quantum Human Design gives you the chance to explore the parts of your chart that are "defined" and "undefined"—the parts of your unique human story—and learn how to consciously choose your own personal narrative beyond your life experiences and your conditioning.

The story you tell yourself regarding "who you think you are" sets the tone and the direction for your life. If you want to change your life path, you have to tell a new story about yourself.

My intention for creating these cards is to give you a concrete and easy way to explore how you can create a personal narrative that truly serves you. I want you to tell a story about yourself that reflects the truth about how creative, how intelligent, how resourceful, how resilient and how powerful you really are. (Because you are!)

The information on these cards give you a systematic way to explore elements of your current story that may be limiting what you are allowing yourself to create. These cards are a tool to give you a concrete strategy to begin rewriting your personal narrative that supports you in fulfilling your true potential!

Whether or not you have these Gates "defined" on your Quantum Human Design chart (colored) or "undefined" (white), you still have all of these energies within you. The Quantum Human Design Activation cards give you an ordered way to consciously contemplate and choose how you will express the highest possible expression of all of these archetypes (or different components or descriptions of aspects of human potential).

You are about to embark on a journey that will change your life!

When you use these archetypes to choose a personal narrative deeply aligned with your vital, unique and irreplaceable role in the cosmic plan, you not only change the direction of your life, you help make the world more whole.

Thank you.

From my Heart to Yours,

Karen

How to Work with the Cards

These cards are meant to be a form of self-reflection, expansion and discovery so you can be aware of what you need to do to deepen your alignment with your Authentic Self paired with the natural flow of support the Universe is seeking to send you. When you align with Who You Truly Are, you activate a rain of support that helps you continue your personal growth and the expansion of the fulfillment of your right place of service to the world.

When you are aligned and living from your Authentic Identity, you increase the possibility of experiencing deeper states of well-being in every area of your life. You also model for others how to live in authentic alignment.

Your state of alignment minimizes resistance and allows you to increase your frequency of energy. This aligned state not only demonstrates to others the fulfillment of your Authentic Self, but also creates an energy wave that supports others in claiming their own Authentic Selves.

The cards represent an aspect of your consciousness that is supporting you in fulfilling the full potential of your Authentic Self. You are entering into a relationship with these cards. Take some time to hold them, set your intention to use them to support your personal growth as well as your evolution so you can truly make them your own in a way that feels good to you.

Each card represents an archetype from Quantum Human Design. These archetypes are the synthesis of ancient and modern expressions that help decipher the components of our human experience. Each of these archetypes gives us an invitation to explore what we need to do to live out the highest expression of our True Selves.

Archetypes are simply a neutral description of a human potential. Your personal narrative is comprised of all of the archetypes in your Quantum Human Design chart. It is the meaning you give archetypes that yields direction to your life story. Every human archetype can be experienced on a spectrum of potential.

For example, let's consider Gate 1, the Gate of Purpose. In its highest expression, the Gate of Purpose is the ability to know the Authentic Self and to live aligned with a deep connection with a Life Purpose. The lowest or unbalanced expression of this Gate is to live a purposeless life and to feel disconnected from any meaning or direction. How you give direction to your life with the meaning of Gate 1, the Gate of Purpose, is how the energy is expressed in your unique story.

Most of us express somewhere along the midpoint of possibility on the spectrum of potential for each archetype. With awareness and understanding, you can learn to consciously choose the highest expression of each archetype.

In fact, we all have all of the Gates in the Quantum Human Design chart. You will have Gates "defined" (colored) on your chart, which represent a consistent theme that we work with to master over the course of our lives. But even when Gates are open or "undefined" (white), they are still present and their energies resonate with our defined gates that we express more purposefully from the energy we absorbed or have learned to use more fully.

Learning tools abound, but I created these cards for you to use to reach your highest Authentic Self. For example, you can use these cards as a tool or an "oracle" of sorts to give you insights into specific challenges in your life. You can also use them as part of a conscious practice to help you deepen your self-mastery and your ability to consciously choose to express your best Self. You may even consider them a mechanism to help you learn about other's strengths to help them shine brighter, too.

Each card has the image and the name of a Quantum Human Design Gate. Once you pull a card, refer to this booklet for the meaning of the card.

Each explanation of the card has five categories for contemplation and self-exploration:

1. **The Challenge:** *Represents what needs to be learned in order to fulfill the highest expression of the Gate theme.*

2. **Mastery:** *The highest potential expression of the energy of the Gate.*

3. **Unbalanced Expression:** *What you might be struggling with or how you might be expressing the Gate if you have lessons to learn from this archetype.*

4. **Affirmation:** *Each Gate has an affirmation, an expression of the positive potential of the Gate's energy. It helps you solidify your intentions when you write the affirmation in your own handwriting. If you post it somewhere you will notice it, this serves to remind yourself of what your focus should be (or "work-in-progress") and how you want to choose to express this archetype.*

5. **Resiliency Keys:** *At the root of every archetype in the Quantum Human Design chart are nine core archetypes called the Resiliency Keys. These nine Keys are often triggered when we are learning from or are challenged by a Gate archetype.*

When you are living the highest expression of each of these core archetypes, you become more resilient. You are able to flow and stay connected with your Authentic Self no matter what life adventure you may be facing.

Some Gates have more than one Resiliency Key associated with them. When you use the cards, note the Resiliency Keys associated with each Gate. Working with not only the Gate theme but also with the Resiliency Keys associated with the Gate supports you in consciously choosing the highest expression of the archetype of the Gate.

When contemplating a specific Gate, it helps to reference the Resiliency Keys associated with the Gate and work with the following questions along with your contemplations of the Gate:

THE NINE RESILIENCY KEYS ARE:

1. **Lovability:** *How much love you believe you can receive, experience and give. What needs to be healed, released, aligned and brought to my awareness for me to be completely open to giving and receiving love?*

2. **Authenticity:** *How free you feel to fully express your Authentic Self. What needs to be healed, released, aligned and brought to my awareness for me to fully express my Authentic Identity?*

3. **Courage:** *How well you are able to navigate through fear without letting it paralyze you. What needs to be healed, released, aligned and brought to my awareness for me to move forward with courage and faith?*

4. **Emotional Wisdom:** *Your ability to use emotional energy as a creative source of power and to be deliberate, not reactive, with emotional energy. What needs to be healed, released, aligned and brought to my awareness in order for me to be a powerful, deliberate Creator? What needs to be healed, released, aligned and brought to my awareness for me to trust my emotional energy? What needs to be healed, released, aligned and brought to my awareness for me to ask for what I want and need?*

5. **Decisiveness:** *Your ability to know how to make decisions that are good and right for you. What needs to be healed, released, aligned and brought to my awareness for me to make clear and strong choices?*

6. **Self-Trust:** *The degree to which you trust your inner wisdom and trust in your own abilities. What needs to be healed, released, aligned and brought to my awareness in order for me to trust myself and my inner knowing?*

7. **Self-Worth:** *Your self-esteem and your sense of your own value. What needs to be healed, released, aligned and brought to my awareness in order for me to fully proclaim my preciousness?*

8. **Vitality:** *How much energy you have to do the things you want and need to do in your life. What needs to be healed, released, aligned and brought to my awareness for me to heal from this burnout?*

9. **Empowerment:** *How much control and power you feel like you have over creating your life. What needs to be healed, released, aligned and brought to my awareness for me to fully own and express my power?*

You can take these contemplations into your meditation,

journal with them or even read them to yourself before you go to bed at night in order to dream on them.

Always work with the cards with loving curiosity and non-judgement towards yourself. The purpose of this exploration is to raise your frequency of energy and to give you greater choice over how you want to express and experience your personal narrative. These cards are not like traditional oracle or tarot cards; these cards help you gain influence over your own future.

Before you use the cards, give yourself time and create a space for you to have the freedom to contemplate the ideas that each card is giving you. Take a moment before you pull a card and ask the following question:

"What needs to be healed, released, aligned or brought to my awareness for me to choose the highest possible outcome for this situation?"

When it feels right, draw a card and begin to explore the message the card holds for you.

You can also choose a daily card as a way of focusing your intention for the day. Simply ask the following question and then pull your card for the day:

"What needs to be healed, released, aligned or brought to my awareness for me to create a day that is the manifestation of my highest purpose and intention?"

When you use these cards with the accompanying questions, you set yourself up to receive deep insights, awareness and a new set of choices. You are choosing to help yourself fully actualize and activate your creativity and the highest expression of your Authentic Self.

Have fun!

Gate 1: Purpose

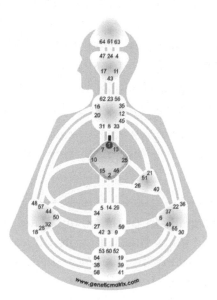

Challenge:

To discover a personal, meaningful and world-changing narrative that aligns with a sense of purpose and mission. "I am..." To learn to love yourself enough to honor the idea that your life is the canvas and you are the artist. What you create with your life IS the contribution you give the world.

Mastery:

The ability to know the Authentic Self and a deep connection with a Life Purpose.

Unbalanced Expression:

An erratic or purposeless life, panic and a feeling of "failing" at a life "mission", pressure to create something unique in the world, struggle to find purpose, hiding because the purpose feels too big, too much or "egotistical".

Resiliency Keys:

Lovability: *What needs to be healed, released, aligned and brought to my awareness for me to be completely open to giving and receiving love?*

Decisiveness: *What needs to be healed, released, aligned and brought to my awareness for me to make clear and strong choices?*

Courage: *What needs to be healed, released, aligned and brought to my awareness for me to move forward with courage and faith?*

Authenticity: *What needs to be healed, released, aligned and brought to my awareness for me to fully express my Authentic Identity?*

Affirmation:

My life is an integral part of the cosmos and the Divine Plan. I honor my life and know that being the full expression of who I am is the purpose of my life. The more I am who I am, the more I create a frequency of energy that supports others in doing the same. I commit to exploring all of who I am.

Further Contemplations:

1. *Am I fully expressing my authentic self?*
2. *What needs to be healed, released, aligned or brought to my awareness for me to more deeply express my authentic self?*
3. *Where am I already expressing who I am?*
4. *Where have I settled or compromised? What needs to change?*
5. *Do I feel connected to my life purpose? What do I need to do to deepen that connection?*

Gate 2: Allowing

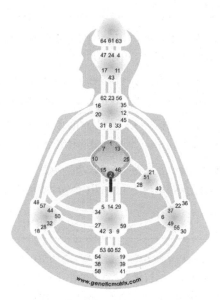

Challenge:

To love yourself enough to open to the flow of support, love and abundance. To incrementally increase over the course of your life what you're willing to allow yourself to receive. To learn to know that you are valuable and lovable simply because you exist.

Mastery:

To set intentions and move solidly towards the fulfillment of the Authentic Self with complete trust that you are supported in being the full expression of who you are and your life purpose, even if you don't know how or what the support will look like. Trust in Source. Living in a state of gratitude.

Unbalanced Expression:

To experience stress, fear and ultimately compromise on what you want and who you are because you don't trust that you are supported. To be valiantly self-sufficient to the point of burning yourself out. To never ask for help.

Resiliency Keys:

Lovability: *What needs to be healed, released, aligned and brought to my awareness for me to love myself better?*

Decisiveness: *What needs to be healed, released, aligned and brought to my awareness for me to make clear and strong choices?*

Courage: *What needs to be healed, released, aligned and brought to my awareness for me to move forward with courage and faith?*

Authenticity: *What needs to be healed, released, aligned and brought to my awareness for me to fully express my Authentic Identity?*

Affirmation:

I allow myself to receive the full flow of resources and abundance I need to fully express all of who I am. I recognize that my life is a vital, irreplaceable part of the cosmic tapestry and I receive all that I need because it helps me contribute all that I am.

Further Contemplations:

1. *Do I ask for help when I need it? Why or why not?*
2. *Do I trust the Universe/God/Spirit/Source to support me in fulfilling my intentions?*
3. *Am I grateful for what I have? (Make a list of everything I am grateful for.)*
4. *Can I transform my worry into trust?*
5. *Do I believe that I deserve to be supported?*

Gate 3: Innovation

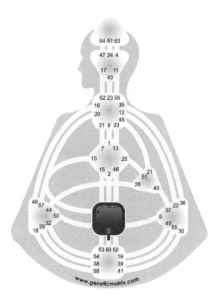

Challenge:

To learn to trust in Divine Timing and to know that your ideas and insights will be transmitted to the world when the world is ready.

Mastery:

The ability to embrace and integrate new ideas and new ways of doing things. To learn to stay in appreciation for your unique way of thinking and being and to trust that, as an innovator on the leading edge of consciousness, your time to transmit what you're here to bring forth will come, so you wait and cultivate your ideas with patience.

Unbalanced Expression:

To feel pressured and panicked about the need to share an idea or innovation. To burn yourself out trying to override Divine Timing.

Resiliency Keys:

Vitality: *What needs to be healed, released, aligned and brought to my awareness for me to heal from this burnout?*

Decisiveness: *What needs to be healed, released, aligned and brought to my awareness for me to make clear and strong choices?*

Courage: *What needs to be healed, released, aligned and brought to my awareness for me to move forward with courage and faith?*

Empowerment: *What needs to be healed, released, aligned and brought to my awareness for me to feel powerful in this situation?*

Affirmation:

I am here to bring change to the world. My natural ability to see what else is possible to create something new is my strength and my gift. I patiently cultivate my inspiration, and use my understanding of what is needed to help evolve the world.

Further Contemplations:

1. *Where has Divine Timing worked out in my life? What has waiting taught me?*

2. *Do I trust in Divine Timing?*

3. *If the opportunity to share my ideas with the world presented itself today, would I be ready? If not, what do I need to prepare to be ready?*

Gate 4: Possibility

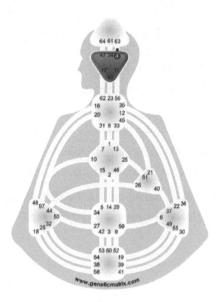

www.geneticmatrix.com

Challenge:

To learn to embrace ideas as possibilities, not answers, and to let the power of the possibility stimulate the imagination as a way of calibrating the emotions and the Heart. This Gate teaches us the power of learning to wait and see which possibility actually manifests in the physical world and to experiment with options in response.

This Gate also teaches us not to be doubtful if the idea isn't manifesting immediately, or to turn doubt inward if you can't figure out how to make this idea a reality.

Mastery:

The ability to experience an idea as a possibility, to learn to use the idea as a "seed" for the imagination and to use the imagination to create an emotional response which then calibrates the

Heart and attracts experiences and opportunities that match the possibility into your life.

Unbalanced Expression:

Self-doubt and fear that you have an idea that you can't figure out. The pressure to try to share or implement the idea before it has had time to "seed" the manifestation. Acting too soon without waiting for the right timing.

Resiliency Keys:

Self-trust: *What needs to be healed, released, aligned and brought to my awareness in order for me to trust myself and my inner knowing?*

Decisiveness: *What needs to be healed, released, aligned and brought to my awareness for me to make clear and strong choices?*

Affirmation:

I am tuned into the cosmic flow of possibility. I am inspired about exploring new possibilities and potentials. I use the power of my thoughts to stretch the limits of what is known and engage my imagination to explore the potential of the unknown.

Further Contemplations:

1. *What ideas do I have right now that need me to nurture and activate them?*

2. *What possibilities do these ideas stimulate right now? Take some time to write or visualize these possibilities.*

3. *Am I comfortable with waiting? What can I do to increase my patience and curiosity?*

Gate 5: Consistency

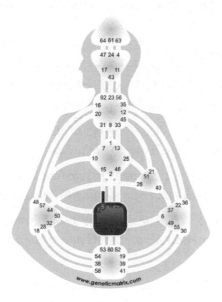

Challenge:

To learn to craft order, habits and rhythm that support alignment, connection and the flow of Life Force energy and the fulfillment of purpose. To master staying in tune with consistent habits and alignment that support your growth and evolution no matcr what is going on around you. Aligning with natural order and staying attuned to the unfolding of the flow of the natural world.

Mastery:

The ability to stay consistent with habits and choices that bring you closer to living true to who you are through alignment, and not overusing will power.

Unbalanced Expression:

Life will seem like a constant struggle to stay connected and live habitually in a way that creates stability, sustainability and a fulfilled expression.

Resiliency Keys:

Vitality: *What needs to be healed, released, aligned and brought to my awareness for me to heal from this burnout?*

Decisiveness: *What needs to be healed, released, aligned and brought to my awareness for me to make clear and strong choices?*

Courage: *What needs to be healed, released, aligned and brought to my awareness for me to move forward with courage and faith?*

Empowerment: *What needs to be healed, released, aligned and brought to my awareness for me to feel powerful in this situation?*

Affirmation:

Consistency gives me power. When I am aligned with my own natural rhythm and the rhythm of life around me I cultivate strength, connection with Source, and I am a beacon of stability and order. The order I hold is the touchstone, the returning point of love, that is sustained through cycles of change. The rhythms I maintain set the standard for compassionate action in the world.

Further Contemplations:

1. *What do I need to do to create habits that fuel my energy and keep me vital and feeling connected to myself and Source?*

2. *What habits do I have that might not be serving my highest expression? How can I change those habits?*

3. *What kind of environment do I need to cultivate to support my rhythmic nature?*

Gate 6: Impact

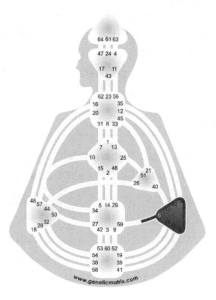

Challenge:

The ability to master emotional energy and learn to trust that your impact is in service to the world. When you understand that your life is a vehicle for service and your energy is being used to influence and impact those around you, you assume greater obligation and responsibility to maintaining a high frequency of energy. The quality of the emotional energy you cultivate influences others to come together in an equitable, sustainable and peaceful way. Learning to trust that your words and impact will have effect when the timing is correct and not overriding Divine Timing.

Mastery:

Maintaining a high frequency of emotional energy that supports equitability, sustainability and peace. Using your emotional alignment to influence others and to serve as an energetic beacon of peace.

Unbalanced Expression:

Feeling desperate, emotionally reactive, lacking and invisible, and being willing to do whatever it takes to take resources and energy for your own good, regardless of the means. Fear that you'll never be seen or heard.

Resiliency Keys:

Courage: *What needs to be healed, released, aligned and brought to my awareness for me to move forward with courage and faith?*

Emotional Wisdom: *What needs to be healed, released, aligned and brought to my awareness in order for me to be a powerful, deliberate Creator? What needs to be healed, released, aligned and brought to my awareness for me to trust my emotional energy? What needs to be healed, released, aligned and brought to my awareness for me to ask for what I want and need?*

Empowerment: *What needs to be healed, released, aligned and brought to my awareness for me to feel powerful in this situation?*

Decisiveness: *What needs to be healed, released, aligned and brought to my awareness for me to make clear and strong choices?*

Affirmation:

My emotional energy influences the world around me. I am rooted in the energy of equity, sustainability and peace. When I am aligned with abundance, I am an energetic source of influence that facilitates elegant solutions to creating peace and wellbeing. I am deliberate and aligned with values that create peace in my life, in my community and in the world.

Further Contemplations:

1. *What do I need to do to deepen my trust in Divine Timing?*

2. *What do I need to do to prepare myself to be seen and to have influence?*

3. *What do I need to do to sustain my emotional energy in order to align with peaceful and sustainable solutions?*

4. *How do I feel about lack? How do I feel about abundance? How can I create a greater degree of emotional abundance in my life? In my daily practice?*

Gate 7: Collaboration

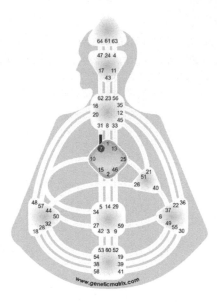

Challenge:

To master the need to be in front and allow yourself to serve through building teams, collaborating and influencing the figurehead of leadership. To be at peace with serving the leader through support and collaboration. To recognize that the voice of the leader is only as strong and powerful as the support he/she receives.

Mastery:

To embrace that power comes from supporting, influencing and collaborating with leadership. To recognize that you don't have to be the figurehead to influence the direction that leadership assumes. The chief of staff is often more powerful than the president. The energy to unify people around an idea that influences the direction of leadership.

Unbalanced Expression:

To struggle and fight to be seen and recognized as the leader at cost to your energy and the fulfillment of your purpose.

Resiliency Keys:

Lovability: *What needs to be healed, released, aligned and brought to my awareness for me to love myself better?*

Decisiveness: *What needs to be healed, released, aligned and brought to my awareness for me to make clear and strong choices?*

Courage: *What needs to be healed, released, aligned and brought to my awareness for me to move forward with courage and faith?*

Authenticity: *What needs to be healed, released, aligned and brought to my awareness for me to fully express my Authentic Identity?*

Affirmation:

I am an agent of peace who influences the direction and organization of leadership. I unify people around ideas. I influence with my wisdom, my knowledge and my connections. I am a team builder, a collaborator, and I organize people in ways that empower them and support them in creating a collective direction rooted in compassion.

Further Contemplations:

1. *What are my gifts and strengths? How do I use those gifts to influence and lead others?*

2. *How do I feel about not being the figurehead of leadership? What happens when I "only" support the leadership? Do I still feel powerful? Influential?*

3. *Make a list of the times when my influence has positively directed leadership?*

Gate 8: Fulfillment

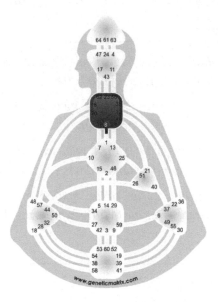

Challenge:

To learn to express yourself authentically. To wait for the right people to see the value of who you are, and to share yourself with them vulnerably with all your heart. To learn to trust that you are a unique expression of the Divine with a purpose and a path. To find that path and to walk it without self-judgement or holding back.

Mastery:

To push the edges and boundaries of authentic self-expression and to realize that you being the full expression of your authentic self IS your life purpose. To use your authentic expression to inspire others to fulfill themselves.

Unbalanced Expression:

Feeling panicked and disconnected from your Life Purpose. Thinking that your Life Purpose is something you have to "do" versus someone you have to "be". To try to be someone you're not in an attempt to serve as a "role model".

Resiliency Keys:

Authenticity: *What needs to be healed, released, aligned and brought to my awareness for me to fully express my Authentic Identity?*

Vitality: *What needs to be healed, released, aligned and brought to my awareness for me to heal from this burnout?*

Affirmation:

I am devoted to the full expression of who I am. I defend and protect the story of my Life. I know that when I am expressing myself, without hesitation or limitation, I AM the contribution that I am here to give the world. Being myself IS my life purpose and my direction flows from my authentic alignment.

Further Contemplations:

1. *Do I feel safe being vulnerable? What experiences have caused me to feel unsafe expressing my true self? Can I rewrite those stories?*

2. *What would an uncompromising life look like for me?*

3. *What do I need to remove from my current life to make my life more authentic?*

4. *What is one bold action I can take right now that would allow me to express who I am more authentically in the world? What is my true passion? What do I dream of?*

Gate 9: Convergence

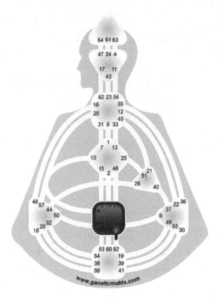

www.geneticmatrix.com

Challenge:

This energy is about learning where to place your focus. When we work with the energy of this Gate, we have to learn to see the trees AND the forest. This Gate can make us seem "blind" to the big picture and we can lose our focus by getting stuck going down a "rabbit hole".

Mastery:

The ability to see the "big picture" and be able to prioritize where to focus your energy.

Unbalanced Expression:

Feeling pressured to figure out where to place your focus. Feeling overwhelmed and confused by too many options and choices. Not being able to see the relationship between ideas and actions and missing the important details.

Resiliency Keys:

Vitality: *What needs to be healed, released, aligned and brought to my awareness for me to heal from this burnout?*

Decisiveness: *What needs to be healed, released, aligned and brought to my awareness for me to make clear and strong choices?*

Courage: *What needs to be healed, released, aligned and brought to my awareness for me to move forward with courage and faith?*

Empowerment: *What needs to be healed, released, aligned and brought to my awareness for me to feel powerful in this situation?*

Affirmation:

I place my focus and attention on the details that support my creative manifestation. I am clear. I easily see the parts of the whole and I know exactly what to focus on to support my evolution and the evolution of the world.

Further Contemplations:

1. *Where am I putting my energy and attention? Is it creating the growth that I am seeking?*
2. *What do I need to focus on?*
3. *Is my physical environment supporting me in staying focused?*
4. *Do I have a practice that supports me in sustaining my focus? What can I do to increase my focus?*

Gate 10: Self-Love

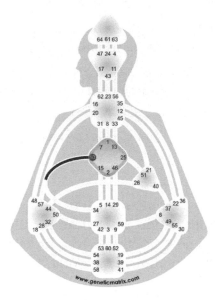

Challenge:

To learn to love yourself. To learn to take responsibility for your own creations.

Mastery:

To see your love for yourself as the source of your true creative power.

Unbalanced Expression:

To question your lovability, struggle to prove your love-worthiness, to give up and settle for less than what you deserve and to blame others for your circumstances and situations. Victim consciousness.

Resiliency Keys:

Lovability: *What needs to be healed, released, aligned and brought to my awareness for me to love myself better?*

Decisiveness: *What needs to be healed, released, aligned and brought to my awareness for me to make clear and strong choices?*

Courage: *What needs to be healed, released, aligned and brought to my awareness for me to move forward with courage and faith?*

Authenticity: *What needs to be healed, released, aligned and brought to my awareness for me to fully express my Authentic Identity?*

Affirmation:

I am an individuated aspect of the Divine. I am born of Love. My nature is to Love and be Loved. I am in the full flow of giving and receiving Love. I know that the quality of Love that I have for myself, sets the direction for what I attract into my life. I am constantly increasing the quality of love I experience and share with the world.

Further Contemplations:

1. *Do I love myself?*
2. *What can I do to deepen my self-love?*
3. *Where can I find evidence of my lovability in my life right now?*
4. *What do I need to do to take responsibility for situations I hate in my life right now? What needs to change?*
5. *Where am I holding blame or victimhood in your life? How could I turn that energy around?*

Gate 11: The Conceptualist

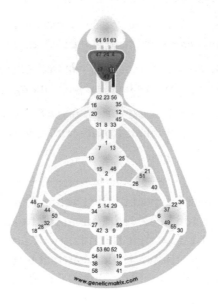

Challenge:

To sort through and manage all the ideas and inspiration you hold. To trust that the ideas that are yours will show up for you in an actionable way. To value yourself enough to value the ideas you have and to wait for the right people to share those ideas with.

Mastery:

The awareness that you are a vessel for ideas. To understand that those ideas are for you to hold and protect until the right person comes along for you to share them with. To relax as the vessel and know that not all ideas are yours to build upon. To use the power of your inspiration to stimulate the imagination of yourself and others.

Unbalanced Expression:

Desperately trying to force every idea you have into manifestation.

Resiliency Keys:

Decisiveness: *What needs to be healed, released, aligned and brought to my awareness for me to make clear and strong choices?*

Self-Trust: *What needs to be healed, released, aligned and brought to my awareness in order for me to trust myself and my inner knowing?*

Affirmation:

I am a Divine Vessel of inspiration. Ideas flow to me constantly. I protect and nurture these ideas knowing that my purpose in life is to share ideas and inspiration with others. I use the power of these ideas to stimulate my imagination and the imagination of others. I trust the infinite abundance and alignment of the Universe and I wait for signs to know which ideas are mine to manifest.

Further Contemplations:

1. *What do I do with inspiration when I receive it? Do I know how to serve as a steward for my ideas? Or do I feel pressure to try to force them into form?*

2. *How much do I value myself? Am I valuing my ideas?*

3. *Do I trust the Universe? Do I trust that the ideas that are mine to take action on will manifest in my life according to my Human Design Type and Strategy?*

4. *What can I do to manage the pressure I feel to manifest my ideas? Am I trying to prove my value with my ideas?*

Gate 12: The Channel

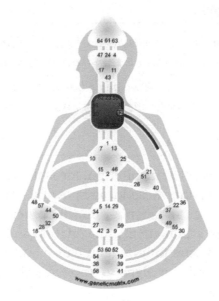

Challenge:

To honor the self enough to wait for the right time and "mood" to speak. To know that "shyness" is actually a signal that the timing isn't right to share your transformational insights and expressions. When the timing IS right, to have the courage to share what you feel and sense. To honor the fact that your voice and the words you offer are a direct connection to Source and you channel the potential for transformation. To own your creative power.

Mastery:

To know that your voice is an expression of transformation and a vehicle for Divine Insight. The words you speak, the insights and creativity you share have the power to change others and the world. This energy is so powerful that people have to be ready to receive it. When you are articulate, then the timing is correct.

If you struggle to find the words, have the courage to wait until it feels more aligned. A powerful ability to craft language and creative expressions that changes people's perceptions.

Unbalanced Expression:

The struggle to try to speak ideas into form when it's not the right time. Letting hesitancy and caution paralyze you. Trying to force ideas and words.

Resiliency Keys:

Authenticity: *What needs to be healed, released, aligned and brought to my awareness for me to fully express my Authentic Identity?*

Vitality: *What needs to be healed, released, aligned and brought to my awareness for me to heal from this burnout?*

Affirmation:

I am a creative being. My words, my self-expression, my creative offerings have the power to change the way people see and understand the world. I am a vessel of Divine Transformation and I serve Source through the words that I share. I wait for the right timing and when I am aligned with timing and flow, my creativity creates beauty and Grace in the world. I am a Divine Channel and I trust that the words that I serve will open the Hearts of others.

Further Contemplations:

1. *How has "shyness" caused me to judge myself?*
2. *What do I need to do to cultivate a deeper connection with Source?*
3. *What do I need to do to connect more deeply with my creative power?*

Gate 13: Narrative

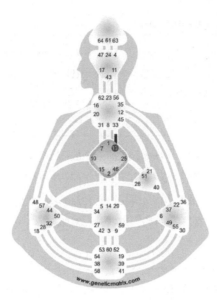

Challenge:

To forgive the past and redefine who you are each and every day. To tell a personal narrative that is empowering, self-loving and reflects your value and your authentic self. To bear witness to the pain and narrative of others and offer them a better story that allows them to expand on their abundance and blessings.

Mastery:

The ability to use the power of personal narrative to create with power and intention.

Unbalanced Expression:

Staying stuck in old stories. Holding on to old past pains. Staying the victim in a story that repeats itself because your personal narrative is stuck in an old story.

Resiliency Keys:

Lovability: *What needs to be healed, released, aligned and brought to my awareness for me to love myself better?*

Decisiveness: *What needs to be healed, released, aligned and brought to my awareness for me to make clear and strong choices?*

Courage: *What needs to be healed, released, aligned and brought to my awareness for me to move forward with courage and faith?*

Authenticity: *What needs to be healed, released, aligned and brought to my awareness for me to fully express my Authentic Identity?*

Affirmation:

The story that I tell myself and the world that I am, sets the tone and the direction for my life. I am the artist and creator of my story. I have the power to rewrite my story every day. The true story I tell from my Heart allows me to serve my Right Place in the Cosmic Plan.

Further Contemplations:

1. *What stories about my life am I holding on to?*
2. *Do these stories reflect who I really am and what I really want to be creating with my life?*
3. *What or who do I need to forgive in order to liberate myself to tell a new story?*
4. *What secrets or stories am I holding for others? Do I need to release them?*
5. *Write the true story of who I really am...*

Gate 14: Creation

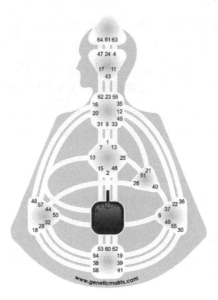

Challenge:

To learn to trust to respond to opportunities that bring resources instead of forcing them or overworking. To learn to value resources and to appreciate how easily they can be created when you are aligned. To be gracious and grateful and not take for granted the resources you have.

Mastery:

The ability to be at peace about having resources. To be in a constant state of trust that everything you need will show up in your outer reality in accordance with your alignment with Source. The resources you have allow you to increase the resources for others. To change the definition of "work". To no longer work for material gain, but work for the sake of transforming the world and being in the flow of life. To know that support flows from alignment with your Heart.

Unbalanced Expression:

Fear and worry about money. Being willing to compromise your "right" work to do whatever you have to do for material gain.

Resiliency Keys:

Decisiveness: *What needs to be healed, released, aligned and brought to my awareness for me to make clear and strong choices?*

Courage: *What needs to be healed, released, aligned and brought to my awareness for me to move forward with courage and faith?*

Vitality: *What needs to be healed, released, aligned and brought to my awareness for me to heal from this burnout?*

Empowerment: *What needs to be healed, released, aligned and brought to my awareness for me to feel powerful in this situation?*

Affirmation:

I am in the flow of Divine Support. When I trust the generous nature of the Divine and I cultivate a state of faith, I receive all the opportunities and support that I need to evolve my life and transform the world. I know that the right work shows up for me and I am fulfilled in the expression of my life force energy.

Further Contemplations:

1. *Do I trust that I am supported?*

2. *Am I doing my "right" work? What is the work that feels aligned with my purpose? How is that work showing up in my life right now?*

3. *What resources do I have right now that I need to be grateful for?*

4. *If I didn't "need" the money, what work would I be doing?*

Gate 15: Compassion

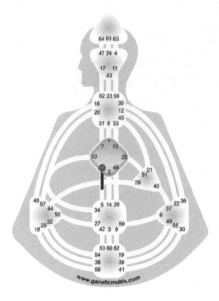

Challenge:

To learn to allow yourself to be in the flow of your own rhythm. To not beat yourself up because you don't have daily "habits". To have the courage to do the right thing even if you are worried about not having enough. To share from the Heart without giving up your Heart and serving as a "martyr".

Mastery:

The ability to trust your own flow and rhythm, to trust that you will have cycles that disrupt old patterns and force you to re-create your direction and flow. To learn to set parameters for your creativity and work within the parameters when it feels right and then rest in between. Nature has rhythm AND extremes. You are here to change old rhythms and patterns to align them with greater compassion.

Unbalanced Expression:

Self-judgement and extreme habits that are frenetic and non-productive. Trying to force your natural waves of rhythm into the daily practices and habits that society defines as "successful" and struggling with follow-through. Denying your own Heart. Being too afraid to do what feels right.

Resiliency Keys:

Lovability: *What needs to be healed, released, aligned and brought to my awareness for me to love myself better?*

Decisiveness: *What needs to be healed, released, aligned and brought to my awareness for me to make clear and strong choices?*

Courage: *What needs to be healed, released, aligned and brought to my awareness for me to move forward with courage and faith?*

Authenticity: *What needs to be healed, released, aligned and brought to my awareness for me to fully express my Authentic Identity?*

Affirmation:

Like the power of a hurricane to transform the shoreline, my unique rhythm brings change to the landscape of my life and the world around me. I embrace my own rhythm and acknowledge the power of my own Heart. I share with ease and I serve my own Heart as the foundation of all I have to give the world.

Further Contemplations:

1. *Do I trust my own rhythm?*

2. *Do I share from the Heart? Do I over-share? Does my sharing compromise my own Heart?*

3. *Do I judge my own rhythm? Can I find peace in aligning with my own rhythm?*

4. *What old patterns do I need to break?*

Gate 16: Zest

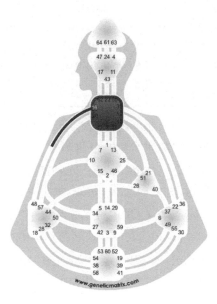

Challenge:

To learn to temper your enthusiasm by making sure you're prepared enough for whatever it is you're trying to do or create.

Mastery:

The courage to leap into action and to inspire others to act, even if you don't know all the details. The courage to trust your own intuition that the timing is right and you are "ready enough" even if you don't know exactly how your journey will unfold. Faith in the outcome.

Unbalanced Expression:

Having a pattern of leaping into the unknown without sufficient preparation. Not assessing whether an idea or inspiration is actually an expression of mastery. "Leaping without looking."

Holding yourself back when you know the time is right because others tell you you're "not ready".

Resiliency Keys:

Authenticity: *What needs to be healed, released, aligned and brought to my awareness for me to fully express my Authentic Identity?*

Vitality: *What needs to be healed, released, aligned and brought to my awareness for me to heal from this burnout?*

Affirmation:

I am a faith-filled contagious force. I take guided actions and I trust my intuition and awareness to let me know when I am prepared and ready to leap into expanding my experience and mastery. My enthusiasm inspires others to trust in themselves and to take their own giant leaps of growth.

Further Contemplations:

1. *Do I trust my "gut"?*
2. *Do I need to slow down and make sure I've done my "homework" before I take action?*
3. *Have I sidelined my enthusiasm because other people have told me that I "can't" do what I'm dreaming of doing?*

Gate 17: Anticipation

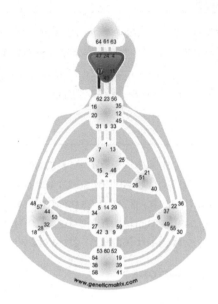

www.geneticmatrix.com

Challenge:

To learn to share your thoughts about possibilities only when people ask for them. To not let doubt and suspicion keep you from seeing the potential of positive outcomes.

Mastery:

To use the power of your mind to explore potentials and possibilities that stretch our ideas about what else is possible in the human condition. To use your thoughts to inspire others to think bigger and bolder. To use your words to inspire and set the stage for creating energy that expands potential.

Unbalanced Expression:

To share opinions that degrade options. To embrace opinions as truth and act on them. To create personal and collective narratives that are negative and filled with doubt.

Resiliency Keys:

Decisiveness: *What needs to be healed, released, aligned and brought to my awareness for me to make clear and strong choices?*

Self-Trust: *What needs to be healed, released, aligned and brought to my awareness in order for me to trust myself and my inner knowing?*

Affirmation:

I use the power of my mind to explore possibilities and potential. I know that my inspirations and insights create exploration and experimentation that can inspire the elegant solutions necessary to master the challenges facing humanity.

Further Contemplations:

1. *What do I need to do to manage my insights and ideas so that they increase the options and potential of others?*

2. *How do I feel about holding back from sharing my insights until the timing is right? What can I do to manage my need to share without waiting for the right timing?*

3. *What routines and strategies do I need to cultivate to keep my perspectives expanding and possibility-oriented?*

4. *How can I improve my ability to manage doubt and fear?*

Gate 18: Re-Alignment

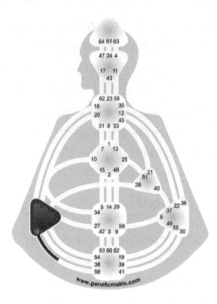

Challenge:

To learn to wait for the right timing and the right circumstances to offer your intuitive insights into how to fix or correct a pattern. To wait for the right time and the right reason to share your critique. To understand that the purpose of re-alignment is to create more joy, not to be "right".

Mastery:

To see a pattern that needs correcting and to wait for the right timing and circumstances to correct and align it. To serve joy.

Unbalanced Expression:

To be critical. To share criticism without respect for the impact. To be more concerned with your own "rightness" than to assess whether your insight is actually adding to more joy in the world.

Resiliency Keys:

Self-Trust: *What needs to be healed, released, aligned and brought to my awareness in order for me to trust myself and my inner knowing?*

Courage: *What needs to be healed, released, aligned and brought to my awareness for me to move forward with courage and faith?*

Affirmation:

I am a powerful force that re-aligns patterns. My insights and awareness gives people the information they need to deepen their mastery and to experience greater joy. I serve joy and I align the patterns of the world to increase the world's potential for living in the flow of joy.

Further Contemplations:

1. *What does joy mean to me? How do I serve it?*

2. *How do I cultivate joy in my own life?*

3. *How does it feel to be "right" about something and keep it to myself? Do I need to release any old "stories" about needing to be "right"?*

4. *Do I trust my own insights? Do I have the courage to share them when it's necessary?*

Gate 19: Attunement

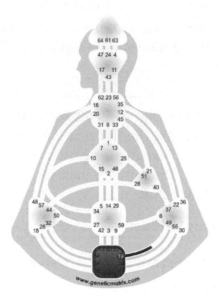

Challenge:

To learn how to manage being a highly sensitive person and not let your sensitivity cause you to compromise what you want and who you are. To learn to keep your own resources in a sustainable state in order so that you have more to give. To not martyr yourself to the needs of others. To learn how to become emotionally intimate without being shut down or co-dependent.

Mastery:

The ability to sense the emotional needs of others and your community, and know how to bring the emotional energy back into alignment with sufficiency and sustainability. The ability to be emotionally vulnerable and present to increase Heart to Heart connections.

Unbalanced Expression:

Being overly sensitive and shutting down or compromising your own needs and wants. Feeling disconnected from others as a way of coping with being overly sensitive. Being emotionally clingy or needy as a way of forcing your natural desire for intimacy.

Resiliency Keys:

Vitality: *What needs to be healed, released, aligned and brought to my awareness for me to heal from this burnout?*

Empowerment: *What needs to be healed, released, aligned and brought to my awareness for me to feel powerful in this situation?*

Affirmation:

I am deeply aware of the emotional needs and energy of others. My sensitivity and awareness gives me insights that allow me to create intimacy and vulnerability in my relationships. I am aware and attuned to the emotional frequency around me and I make adjustments to help support a high frequency of emotional alignment. I honor my own emotional needs as the foundation of what I share with others.

Further Contemplations:

1. *How do I manage my sensitivity? What coping mechanism do I have to keep me emotionally connected in a healthy way?*

2. *Am I emotionally present in my relationships? Do I need to become more attuned to my own emotional needs and ask for more of what I want and need?*

3. *What emotional patterns do I have that may be causing me to give up what I need and want to fulfill other people's emotional needs?*

4. *Am I able to be present to the emotional energy around me to help calibrate in a creative, intimate and sustainable way?*

Gate 20: Patience

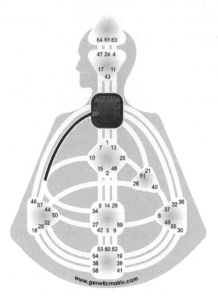

Challenge:

To be patient and master the ability to wait. To be prepared and watchful but resist the urge to act if the timing isn't right, or if there are details that still need to be readied.

Mastery:

The ability to trust your intuition, to know what needs to be set in place, what people need to be gathered, what skills need to be mastered and to be ready when the time is right. To trust in the right timing and to heed the intuition to get ready.

Unbalanced Expression:

To act before the time is right. To fail to listen to your inner guidance and prepare. To feel pressure to take action before the time is right and to feel frustrated or to quit.

Resiliency Keys:

Authenticity: *What needs to be healed, released, aligned and brought to my awareness for me to fully express my Authentic Identity?*

Vitality: *What needs to be healed, released, aligned and brought to my awareness for me to heal from this burnout?*

Affirmation:

I am in the flow of perfect timing. I listen to my intuition. I prepare. I gather the experience, resources and people I need to support my ideas and my principles. When I am ready, I wait patiently, knowing that right timing is the key to transforming the world. My alignment with right timing increases my influence and my power.

Further Contemplations:

1. *How do I manage my need for action? Am I patient? Do I trust in Divine Timing?*

2. *Do I trust my intuition?*

3. *What needs to be healed, released, aligned and brought to my awareness for me to trust my intuition?*

Gate 21: Self-Regulation

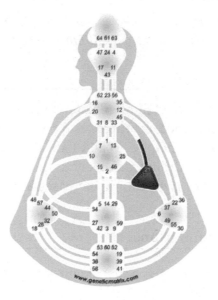

www.geneticmatrix.com

Challenge:

To learn to let go. To master self-regulation. To release the need to control others and circumstances. To trust in the Divine and to know that you are supported. Knowing that you are worthy of support and you don't have to overcompensate.

Mastery:

The ability to regulate your inner and outer environment in order to sustain a vibrational frequency that reflects your true value. The ability to be self-generous and to set boundaries that maintain your value and support you in being sustainable in the world. To take the actions necessary to honor your unique role in the cosmic plan.

Unbalanced Expression:

To feel the need to control life, others, resources, etc. out of fear that you aren't worthy of being supported.

Resiliency Keys:

Self-Worth: *What needs to be healed, released, aligned and brought to my awareness in order for me to fully acknowledge my value?*

Vitality: *What needs to be healed, released, aligned and brought to my awareness for me to heal from this burnout?*

Empowerment: *What needs to be healed, released, aligned and brought to my awareness for me to feel powerful in this situation?*

Affirmation:

I am worthy of claiming, protecting and defending my right place in the world. I create an inner and outer environment that is self-generous and I regulate my environment to sustain a high frequency of alignment with my true value. I know that I am an irreplaceable and precious part of the cosmic plan and I create my life to reflect the importance of my right place in the world.

Further Contemplations:

1. *Where do I need to release control in my life?*

2. *Do I trust the Universe?*

3. *Do I value myself? Do I trust that I'll be supported in accordance with my value?*

4. *What do I need to do to create an internal and external environment of self-generosity?*

5. *What needs to be healed, released, aligned and brought to my awareness for me to embrace my true value?*

Gate 22: Surrender

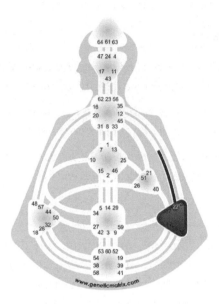

Challenge:

To trust that your passions and deepest desires are supported by the Universal flow of abundance. To have the courage to follow your passion and know that you'll be supported. To learn to regulate your emotional energy so that you have faith that everything will unfold perfectly.

Mastery:

The grace to know that you are fully supported by the Universal flow of abundance and to pursue your passion and your unique contribution to the world no matter what. To trust that you will be given what you need when you need it in order to make your unique contribution to the world.

Unbalanced Expression:

Fear that you are not supported. Holding back or stifling your passion because you think you can't "afford" to pursue it. Compromising, settling or letting despair regulate your emotional energy, causing the creative process to feel shut down or stuck.

Resiliency Keys:

Courage: *What needs to be healed, released, aligned and brought to my awareness for me to move forward with courage and faith?*

Emotional Wisdom: *What needs to be healed, released, aligned and brought to my awareness in order for me to be a powerful, deliberate Creator? What needs to be healed, released, aligned and brought to my awareness for me to trust my emotional energy? What needs to be healed, released, aligned and brought to my awareness for me to ask for what I want and need?*

Empowerment: *What needs to be healed, released, aligned and brought to my awareness for me to feel powerful in this situation?*

Decisiveness: *What needs to be healed, released, aligned and brought to my awareness for me to make clear and strong choices?*

Affirmation:

I am a global change agent. I am inspired with passions that serve the purpose of transforming the world. I trust that my emotions and my passion will align me with faith and the flow of resources I need to fulfill my life purpose. When I let go and follow my passion, I am given everything I need to change the world.

Further Contemplations:

1. *Where am I denying my passion in my life? Where have I settled for less than what I want because I'm afraid I can't get what I want?*

2. *What do I need to do to fully activate my passion? What is one bold step towards my genius that I could take right now?*

3. *Do I trust the Universe? What do I need to do to deepen my trust?*

4. *Do I have a regular practice that supports me in sustaining a high frequency of emotional energy and alignment?*

5. *What needs to be healed, released, aligned and brought to my awareness for me to deepen my faith?*

Gate 23: Transmission

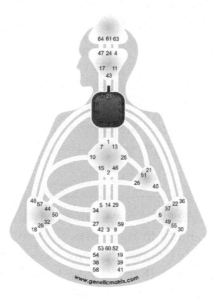

Challenge:

To recognize that change and transformation are inevitable. To know what needs to happen next and to have to wait for the right timing and the right people to share your insights with. To not jump the gun and try to convince people to understand what you know. To not let yourself slip into negativity and despair when people aren't ready.

Mastery:

The ability to be able to translate transformative insights for people that offer them a way to transform the way they think. To share what you know with awareness of right timing, and to trust your knowingness as an expression of your connection to Source.

Unbalanced Expression:

The need to be right. An anxiety or pressure to share what you know with people who aren't ready and then to feel despair or bitterness that they don't understand things the way that you do.

Resiliency Keys:

Authenticity: *What needs to be healed, released, aligned and brought to my awareness for me to fully express my Authentic Identity?*

Vitality: *What needs to be healed, released, aligned and brought to my awareness for me to heal from this burnout?*

Affirmation:

I change the world with what I know. My insights and awarenesses have the ability to transform the way people think and perceive the world. I know that my words are powerful and transformative. I trust that the people who are ready for the change that I bring will ask me for what I know. I am a vessel for my knowingness and I nurture myself while I wait to share what I know.

Further Contemplations:

1. *How can I strengthen my connection to Source?*

2. *Do I trust what I know? What comes up for me when I "know" something but I don't know how I know what I know?*

3. *How do I handle myself when I know something but the people around me aren't ready to hear it yet?*

Gate 24: Blessings

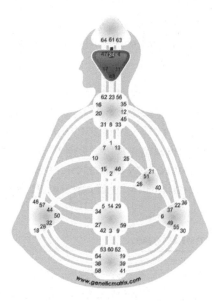

Challenge:

To learn to allow what you truly deserve in your life. To not rationalize allowing less than what you deserve. To find the blessings and power from painful experiences and to use them as catalysts for transformation.

Mastery:

To recognize all experiences have the potential for growth and expansion. To redefine the stories of your experiences to reflect what you learned and how you grew. To be grateful for all of your life experiences and to liberate yourself from stories that no longer serve you.

Unbalanced Expression:

To protect yourself by staying stuck in old patterns. To refuse to transform. To rationalize allowing less than what you deserve.

Resiliency Keys:

Self-Trust: *What needs to be healed, released, aligned and brought to my awareness in order for me to trust myself and my inner knowing?*

Decisiveness: *What needs to be healed, released, aligned and brought to my awareness for me to make clear and strong choices?*

Affirmation:

I embrace the Mystery of Life with the awareness that the infinite generosity of the Universe gives me blessings in every event in my life. I find the blessings from the pain. I grow and expand beyond the limitations of my experiences and stories. I use what I have learned to create a life and circumstances that reflect the miracle that I am.

Further Contemplations:

1. *What are the blessings I learned from my greatest painful experiences? Can I see how these experiences served to teach me? What did I learn?*

2. *What am I grateful for from the past?*

3. *Where might I be rationalizing staying stuck or settling for less than what I really want or deserve? What do I need to do to break out of this pattern?*

Gate 25: Spirit

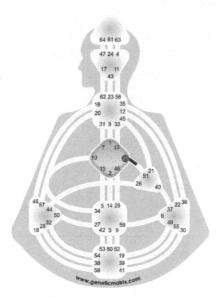

Challenge:

To trust the Divine Order in all of your life. To learn to connect with Source as the path to creating wellbeing in your life. To remember that your life serves an irreplaceable role in the cosmic plan and to honor that role and to live from it. To trust Source.

Mastery:

To connect with Source with consistency and diligence so as to fulfill your Divine Purpose and fulfill the true story of who you are and the role you play in the Cosmic Plan. To use your alignment with Source as a way of healing the world.

Unbalanced Expression:

Fear and mistrust of Spirit. Using your life strictly for personal gains regardless of the impact on others. Ego in the lowest expression. Not feeling worthy of being loved by Source and using your willpower to create instead of alignment.

Resiliency Keys:

Lovability: *What needs to be healed, released, aligned and brought to my awareness for me to love myself better?*

Decisiveness: *What needs to be healed, released, aligned and brought to my awareness for me to make clear and strong choices?*

Courage: *What needs to be healed, released, aligned and brought to my awareness for me to move forward with courage and faith?*

Authenticity: *What needs to be healed, released, aligned and brought to my awareness for me to fully express my Authentic Identity?*

Affirmation:

I am an agent of the Divine. My life is the fulfillment of Divine Order and the Cosmic Plan. When I am connected to Source, I serve my right place. I take up no more than my space and no less than my place in the world. I serve, and through serving, I am supported.

Further Contemplations:

1. *Do I trust Source?*
2. *Do I have a regular practice that connects me to Source?*
3. *Do I know my Life Purpose? Am I living true to my Purpose? How can I deepen my connection to my Purpose?*

Gate 26: Integrity

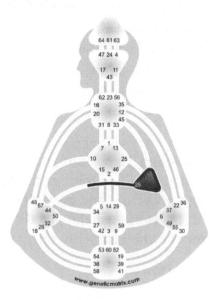

Challenge:

To learn to value your right place and your value enough to act as if you are precious. To heal past traumas and elevate your self-worth. To trust in divine support enough to do the right thing, and to nurture yourself so that you have more to give.

Mastery:

To live in moral, energetic, identity, physical and resource integrity with courage and trust. To set clear boundaries and take the actions necessary to preserve the integrity of your right place.

Unbalanced Expression:

To compromise your integrity because you feel or are afraid that you can't afford to fulfill your right place.

Resiliency Keys:

Self-Worth: *What needs to be healed, released, aligned and brought to my awareness in order for me to fully acknowledge my value?*

Vitality: *What needs to be healed, released, aligned and brought to my awareness for me to heal from this burnout?*

Empowerment: *What needs to be healed, released, aligned and brought to my awareness for me to feel powerful in this situation?*

Affirmation:

I am a unique, valuable and irreplaceable part of the Cosmic Plan. I am always supported in fulfilling my right place. I take care of my body, my energy, my values and my resources so that I have more to share with the world. I claim and defend my value and fully live in the story of who I am with courage.

Further Contemplations:

1. *Where might I be experiencing a breech in my moral, identity, physical, resource or energy integrity? What do I need to do to bring myself back into integrity?*

2. *When I am out of integrity, it can be traumatic. What trauma do I have that I need to heal? How can I rewrite the story of my trauma as an initiation back into my true value?*

3. *What do I need to do right now to nurture myself and to replenish my value?*

Gate 27: Accountability

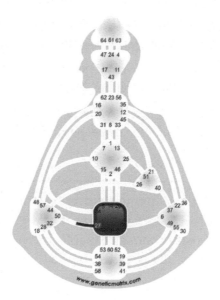

Challenge:

To care without over-caring. To allow others to assume responsibility for their own challenges and choices. To learn to accept other people's values. To not let guilt cause you to compromise what is good and right for you.

Mastery:

The ability to support, nurture and lift others up. To sense and to act on what is necessary to increase the wellbeing of others and the world. To "feed" people with healthy food and healthy nourishment to ensure that they thrive. To hold others accountable for their own self-love and self-empowerment.

Unbalanced Expression:

Co-dependency. Guilt. Over-caring. Martyrdom.

Resiliency Keys:

Decisiveness: *What needs to be healed, released, aligned and brought to my awareness for me to make clear and strong choices?*

Courage: *What needs to be healed, released, aligned and brought to my awareness for me to move forward with courage and faith?*

Vitality: *What needs to be healed, released, aligned and brought to my awareness for me to heal from this burnout?*

Empowerment: *What needs to be healed, released, aligned and brought to my awareness for me to feel powerful in this situation?*

Affirmation:

I have a nurturing and loving nature. It is my gift to be able to love and care for others. I know that the greatest expression of my love is to treat others as capable and powerful. I support when necessary, and I let go with love so that my loved ones can discover their own strength and power.

Further Contemplations:

1. *Am I taking responsibility for things that aren't mine to be responsible for? Whose problem is it? Can I return the responsibility for the problem back to its rightful owner?*

2. *What role does guilt play in motivating me? Can I let go of the guilt? What different choices might I make if I didn't feel guilty?*

3. *What obligations do I need to set down in order for me to take better care of myself?*

4. *Are there places where I need to soften my judgements on other people's values?*

Gate 28: Adventure/Challenge

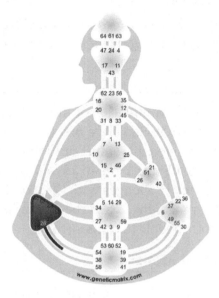

Challenge:

To not let struggle and challenge leave you feeling defeated and despairing. To learn to face life as an adventure. Do not let challenge and struggle cause you to feel as if you've failed.

Mastery:

To learn to share from your personal experience, your struggles and your triumphs. To persevere and to know that the adventures in your life deepen your ability to transform life into a meaningful journey. To understand that your struggles help deepen the collective ideas about what is truly valuable and worthy of creating.

Unbalanced Expression:

Refusing to take action out of fear that the journey will be too painful, wrought with struggle, or that you will fail. To feel like a failure. To fall into victim consciousness.

Resiliency Keys:

Self-trust: *What needs to be healed, released, aligned and brought to my awareness in order for me to trust myself and my inner knowing?*

Courage: *What needs to be healed, released, aligned and brought to my awareness for me to move forward with courage and faith?*

Affirmation:

I am here to push the boundaries of life and what is possible. I thrive in situations that challenge me. I am an explorer on the leading edge of consciousness and my job is to test how far I can go. I embrace challenge. I am an adventurer. I share all that I have learned from my challenges with the world. My stories help give people greater meaning, teach them what is truly worthy of creating and inspire people to transform.

Further Contemplations:

1. *How can I turn my challenge into adventure?*

2. *Where do I need to cultivate a sense of adventure in my life?*

3. *What do I need to do to rewrite the story of my "failures"?*

4. *What meanings, blessings and lessons have I learned from my challenges?*

5. *What needs to be healed, released, aligned and brought to my awareness for me to trust myself and my choices?*

6. *What do I need to do to forgive myself for my perceived past failures?*

Gate 29: Devotion

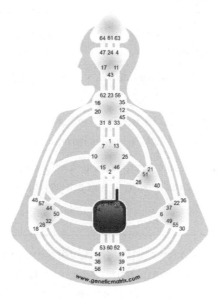

Challenge:

To discover what and who you need to devote yourself too. To sustain yourself so that you can sustain your devotion. To learn to say "no" to what you need to say "no" to, and to learn to say "yes" to what you want to say "yes" to.

Mastery:

The ability to respond to committing to the right thing. To know that your perseverance and determination changes the narrative of the world and shows people what is possible. Your devotion sets the tone for the direction that life takes you.

Unbalanced Expression:

To over-commit. To not know when to let go and when enough is enough. To fail to commit to the right thing. To burn out and deplete yourself because you don't say "yes" to yourself. To do something just because you can, not because you want to.

Resiliency Keys:

Decisiveness: *What needs to be healed, released, aligned and brought to my awareness for me to make clear and strong choices?*

Courage: *What needs to be healed, released, aligned and brought to my awareness for me to move forward with courage and faith?*

Vitality: *What needs to be healed, released, aligned and brought to my awareness for me to heal from this burnout?*

Empowerment: *What needs to be healed, released, aligned and brought to my awareness for me to feel powerful in this situation?*

Affirmation:

I have an extraordinary ability to devote myself to the manifestation of an idea. My commitment to my story and to the fulfillment of my intention changes the story of what's possible in my own life and for humanity. I choose my commitments with great care. I devote myself to what's vital for the evolution of the world, and I nurture myself first because my wellbeing is the foundation of what I create.

Further Contemplations:

1. *What devotion do I have right now that drives me? Is this a devotion that inspires me, or do I feel overly obligated to it?*

2. *Who would I be and what would I choose if I gave myself permission to say "no" more often?*

3. *What would I like to say "no" to that I am saying "yes" to right now?*

4. *What obligations do I need to take off my plate right now?*

5. *What would I like to devote myself to?*

Gate 30: Passion

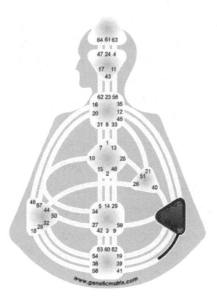

Challenge:

To be able to sustain a dream or a vision without burning out. To know which dream to be passionate about. To not let passion overwhelm you and to wait for the right timing to share your passion with the world.

Mastery:

The ability to sustain a dream, intention and a vision until you bring it into form. To inspire others with the power of your dream. To inspire passion in others.

Unbalanced Expression:

Burnout. Impatience and not waiting for the right timing. Misdirected passion that is perceived as too much intensity. Leaping into chaos.

Resiliency Keys:

Courage: *What needs to be healed, released, aligned and brought to my awareness for me to move forward with courage and faith?*

Emotional Wisdom: *What needs to be healed, released, aligned and brought to my awareness in order for me to be a powerful, deliberate Creator? What needs to be healed, released, aligned and brought to my awareness for me to trust my emotional energy? What needs to be healed, released, aligned and brought to my awareness for me to ask for what I want and need?*

Empowerment: *What needs to be healed, released, aligned and brought to my awareness for me to feel powerful in this situation?*

Decisiveness: *What needs to be healed, released, aligned and brought to my awareness for me to make clear and strong choices?*

Vitality: *What needs to be healed, released, aligned and brought to my awareness for me to heal from this burnout?*

Affirmation:

I am a passionate creator. I use the intensity of my passion to increase my emotional energy and sustain the power of my dream and what I imagine for Life. I trust in the Divine flow and I wait for the right timing and the right circumstances to act on my dream.

Further Contemplations:

1. *What am I passionate about? Have I lost my passion?*

2. *How is my energy? Am I physically burned out? Am I burned out on my ideas?*

3. *What do I need to do to sustain my vision or dream about what I am inspired to create in my life?*

4. *Do I have a dream or vision that I am avoiding because I'm afraid it won't come true?*

Gate 31: The Leader

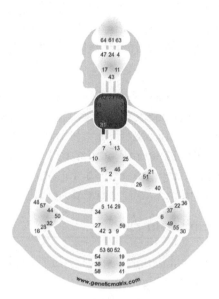

Challenge:

To learn to lead as a representative of the people you are leading. To cultivate a leadership agenda of service. To not let your fear of not being seen, heard or accepted get in the way of healthy leadership. To learn to take your right place as a leader and not hide out.

Mastery:

The ability to be able to listen, learn, hear and serve the people you lead and to assume and value your right leadership position as the voice for the people you are leading.

Unbalanced Expression:

To push and seize leadership for the sake of personal gain, or to be afraid to lead and not feel worthy of serving as a leader.

Resiliency Keys:

Authenticity: *What needs to be healed, released, aligned and brought to my awareness for me to fully express my Authentic Identity?*

Vitality: *What needs to be healed, released, aligned and brought to my awareness for me to heal from this burnout?*

Affirmation:

I am a natural born leader. I serve at my highest potential when I am empowering others by giving them a voice and then serving their needs. I use my power to lead people to a greater expansion of who they are and to support them in increasing their abundance, sustainability and peace.

Further Contemplations:

1. *How do I feel about being a leader? Am I comfortable leading? Do I shrink from taking leadership?*

2. *What is my place of service? Who do I serve?*

Gate 32: Endurance

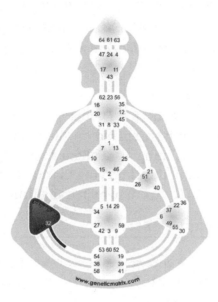

Challenge:

To trust in Divine Timing. To prepare for the next step of manifestation and to align with the unfolding of the process. To be patient.

Mastery:

The awareness of what needs to be done to make a dream a manifested reality. Setting the stage, preparation, being ready. The patience to trust that once the stage is set, the timing will unfold as needed to serve the highest good of all. To translate Divine Inspiration into readiness.

Unbalanced Expression:

Letting the fear of failure cause you to avoid preparing what you need to do. To not be ready when the timing is right. To push too hard, too fast, too long against right timing.

Resiliency Keys:

Self-Trust: *What needs to be healed, released, aligned and brought to my awareness in order for me to trust myself and my inner knowing?*

Courage: *What needs to be healed, released, aligned and brought to my awareness for me to move forward with courage and faith?*

Affirmation:

I am a divine translator for Divine Inspiration. I sense and know what needs to be prepared on the earthly plane in order to be ready for right timing. I am aligned with right timing and I prepare and wait patiently, knowing that when the time is right I will be ready to do the work to help transform pain into power.

Further Contemplations:

1. *What do I need to do to be prepared to manifest my vision? What actionable steps need to be completed in order for me to be ready when the timing is right?*

2. *What do I need to do to cultivate patience?*

3. *Do I have a fear of failing that is causing me to avoid being prepared?*

4. *Am I over-doing and being overly prepared? Am I pushing too hard? What can I let go of?*

Gate 33: Retelling

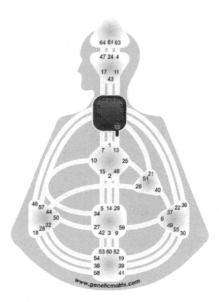

Challenge:

To learn to share a personal narrative that reflects your true value and your worth. To share a personal narrative when it serves the intention of improving the direction of others. To share history in an empowering way.

Mastery:

The ability to translate a personal experience into an empowering narrative that teaches and gives direction to others. Finding the power from the pain. Waiting for the right timing to transform or share a narrative so that it has the greatest impact on the Heart of another.

Unbalanced Expression:

Staying stuck and sharing a personal narrative rooted in pain, disempowerment and victimhood.

Resiliency Keys:

Authenticity: *What needs to be healed, released, aligned and brought to my awareness for me to fully express my Authentic Identity?*

Vitality: *What needs to be healed, released, aligned and brought to my awareness for me to heal from this burnout?*

Affirmation:

I am a processor of stories. My gift is my ability to help others find the blessings, the love and the power from stories of pain. I hold people's secrets and stories and transform them to share when the time is right. The stories I tell change the direction of people's lives. I use the power of stories to increase the power of Heart in the world and to help build a world of Love.

Further Contemplations:

1. *What personal narratives am I telling that might be keeping me stuck, feeling like a victim or feeling unlovable? How can I rewrite these stories?*

2. *What listening practices do I have? What can I do to listen better so that I can gauge when it is the right time to share in a powerful way?*

Gate 34: Power

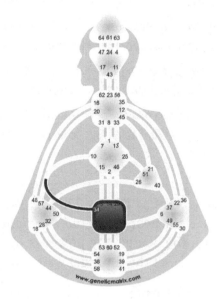

Challenge:

To learn to measure energy in order to stay occupied and busy, but not to burn yourself out trying to force the timing or the "rightness" of a project. To wait to know which project or creation to implement based on when you get something to respond to.

Mastery:

The ability to respond to opportunities to unify the right people around a transformative and powerful idea when the timing and circumstances are correct.

Unbalanced Expression:

Being too busy to tune into the right timing and the right people. Feeling frustrated with pushing and "trying" to make things happen. Forcing manifestation with little results. Depleting yourself because you're pushing too hard.

Resiliency Keys:

Decisiveness: *What needs to be healed, released, aligned and brought to my awareness for me to make clear and strong choices?*

Courage: *What needs to be healed, released, aligned and brought to my awareness for me to move forward with courage and faith?*

Vitality: *What needs to be healed, released, aligned and brought to my awareness for me to heal from this burnout?*

Empowerment: *What needs to be healed, released, aligned and brought to my awareness for me to feel powerful in this situation?*

Affirmation:

I am a powerful servant of Divine Timing. When the timing is right, I unify the right people around the right idea and create transformation on the planet. My power is more active when I allow the Universe to set the timing. I wait. I am patient. I trust.

Further Contemplations:

1. *Do I trust in Divine Timing? What do I need to do to deepen my trust?*

2. *How do I cultivate greater patience in my life?*

3. *What fears come up for me when I think of waiting? How can I learn to wait with greater faith and ease?*

4. *What do I do to occupy myself while I'm waiting?*

Gate 35: Experience

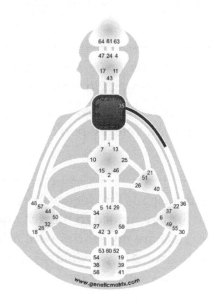

Challenge:

To not let experience lead to feeling jaded or bored. To have the courage to share what you know from your experience. To know which experiences are worth participating in. To not let your natural ability to master anything keep you from being enthusiastic about learning something new. To embrace that even though you know how to know, you don't know everything.

Mastery:

The ability to know which experiences are worthy and worthwhile. To partake in the right experience and to share your knowledge from the experience for the sake of changing the story of what's possible in the world.

Unbalanced Expression:

To be bored with life. To let the boredom of life cause you to settle for a life that never challenges the status quo.

Resiliency Keys:

Authenticity: *What needs to be healed, released, aligned and brought to my awareness for me to fully express my Authentic Identity?*

Vitality: *What needs to be healed, released, aligned and brought to my awareness for me to heal from this burnout?*

Affirmation:

I am an experienced, wise and knowledgeable resource for others. My experiences in life have added to the rich tapestry that is the story of Humanity. I share my stories with others because my experiences open doorways of possibility for others. My stories help others create miracles in their lives.

Further Contemplations:

1. *Where am I finding passion in my life? Do I need to create or discover more passion in my life right now?*

2. *Do I share my knowledge and the stories of my experiences? Do I see the value of what I have to share?*

3. *What am I curious about? How can I expand on that curiosity?*

Gate 36: Exploration

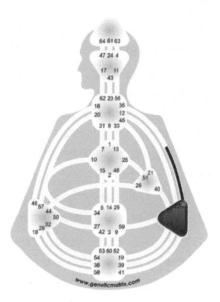

Challenge:

To not let boredom cause you to leap into chaos. To learn to stick with something long enough to become masterful and to bear the fruits of your experience.

Mastery:

The ability to hold a vision and sustain it with an aligned frequency of emotional energy and to bring the vision into form when the timing is right. The ability to stretch the boundaries of the story of Humanity by breaking patterns. Creating miracles through emotional alignment.

Unbalanced Expression:

Not waiting for the right timing and leaping into new opportunities without waiting for alignment, causing chaos. To leap from opportunity to opportunity without waiting to see how the story will play out and never getting to experience the full fruition of the experience.

Resiliency Keys:

Courage: *What needs to be healed, released, aligned and brought to my awareness for me to move forward with courage and faith?*

Emotional Wisdom: *What needs to be healed, released, aligned and brought to my awareness in order for me to be a powerful, deliberate Creator? What needs to be healed, released, aligned and brought to my awareness for me to trust my emotional energy? What needs to be healed, released, aligned and brought to my awareness for me to ask for what I want and need?*

Empowerment: *What needs to be healed, released, aligned and brought to my awareness for me to feel powerful in this situation?*

Decisiveness: *What needs to be healed, released, aligned and brought to my awareness for me to make clear and strong choices?*

Affirmation:

My experiences and stories break old patterns and push the boundaries of the edge of what's possible for humanity. I defy the patterns and I create miracles through my emotional alignment with possibility. I hold my vision and maintain my emotional energy as I wait to bear the fruit of my intentions and my visions.

Further Contemplations:

1. *How does boredom impact my life? What do I do when I feel bored? What can I do to keep myself aligned even when I'm bored?*

2. *What stories have I experienced that have shattered old patterns and expectations? How have my stories changed or inspired others?*

3. *What do I do to maintain or sustain emotional alignment? What do I need to add to my daily practice to "amp" up my emotional energy around my intentions?*

Gate 37: Peace

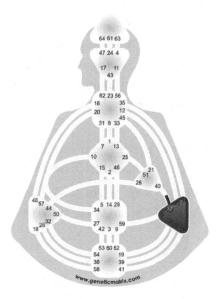

Challenge:

To find inner peace as the true source to outer peace. To not let chaos and outer circumstances knock you off your center and disrupt your peace.

Mastery:

The ability to stay connected to sustainable peace and to respond to life by generating peace no matter what is happening in your external reality. Creating the emotional alignment to make peaceful choices no matter what's going on in the outer world.

Unbalanced Expression:

Desperately struggling to find peace outside of yourself. Trying to control the outer world to create inner peace.

Resiliency Keys:

Courage: *What needs to be healed, released, aligned and brought to my awareness for me to move forward with courage and faith?*

Emotional Wisdom: *What needs to be healed, released, aligned and brought to my awareness in order for me to be a powerful, deliberate Creator? What needs to be healed, released, aligned and brought to my awareness for me to trust my emotional energy? What needs to be healed, released, aligned and brought to my awareness for me to ask for what I want and need?*

Empowerment: *What needs to be healed, released, aligned and brought to my awareness for me to feel powerful in this situation?*

Decisiveness: *What needs to be healed, released, aligned and brought to my awareness for me to make clear and strong choices?*

Affirmation:

I am an agent of peace. My being aligned with peace creates an energy of contagious peace around me. I practice holding a peaceful frequency of energy and I respond to the world with an intention of creating sustainable peace.

Further Contemplations:

1. *What habits, practices and routines do I have that cultivate my inner alignment with sustainable peace?*

2. *When I feel that my outer world is chaotic and disrupted how do I cultivate inner peace?*

3. *What do I need to do to cultivate a peaceful emotional frequency?*

Gate 38: The Visionary

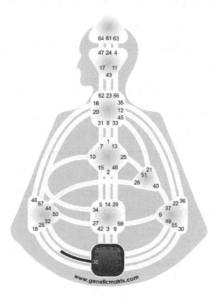

Challenge:

To experience challenge as a way of knowing what's worth fighting for. To turn the story of struggle into a discovery of meaning and to let the power of what you discover serve as a foundation for a strong vision of transformation that brings dreams into manifested form.

Mastery:

The ability to know what's worth committing to and fighting for. To use your experiences to craft a vision that anchors the possibility of something truly meaningful and worthy in the world. Serving the world as a visionary.

Unbalanced Expression:

To struggle and fight for the sake of fighting. Engaging in meaningless fights. Aggression and struggle.

Resiliency Keys:

Vitality: *What needs to be healed, released, aligned and brought to my awareness for me to heal from this burnout?*

Empowerment: *What needs to be healed, released, aligned and brought to my awareness for me to feel powerful in this situation?*

Affirmation:

My challenges, struggles and adventures have taught me about what is truly valuable in life. I use my understandings to hold a vision of what else is possible for the world. I am aligned with the values that reflect the preciousness of life and I sustain a vision for a world that is aligned with Heart. My steadfast commitment to my vision inspires others to join me in creating a world of equitable, sustainable peace.

Further Contemplations:

1. *Do I know what's worth committing to and fighting for in my life?*

2. *Do I have a dream that I am sharing with the world?*

3. *Do I know how to use my struggles and challenges as the catalyst for creating deeper meaning in the world? In my life?*

Gate 39: Recalibration

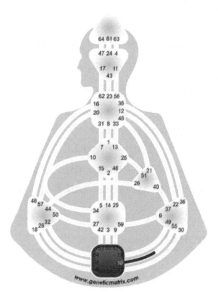

Challenge:

To challenge and tease out energies that are not in alignment with faith and abundance. To bring them to awareness and to use them as pushing off points to deepen faith and trust in Source.

Mastery:

The ability to transform an experience into an opportunity to shift to greater abundance. To see and experience internal or external lack and to use your awareness of lack to re-calibrate your energy towards sufficiency and abundance.

Unbalanced Expression:

Feeling overwhelmed by lack and panicking. Hoarding, over-shopping as a result of fear of lack. Provoking and challenging others and holding others responsible for your own inner alignment with sufficiency.

Resiliency Keys:

Vitality: *What needs to be healed, released, aligned and brought to my awareness for me to heal from this burnout?*

Empowerment: *What needs to be healed, released, aligned and brought to my awareness for me to feel powerful in this situation?*

Affirmation:

I am deeply calibrated with my faith. I trust that I am fully supported. I use experiences that create desire and wanting in me as opportunities to deepen my faith that I will receive and create all that I need to fulfill my mind, body and spirit. I am in the perfect flow of abundance and I am deeply aligned with Source.

Further Contemplations:

1. *Do I trust Source? What do I need to do to deepen my trust in Source?*

2. *Do I feel like I am "enough"? Do I feel like I have "enough"?*

3. *Take stock of everything I have and everything I've been given. Do I have enough? Have I ever really not been supported?*

4. *What do I have that I am grateful for?*

5. *Have I abdicated my own power to create? What needs to be healed, released, aligned or brought to my awareness to reactivate my power to create my own abundance?*

Gate 40: Restoration

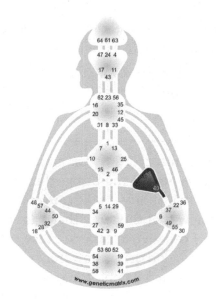

Challenge:

To learn to value yourself enough to retreat from community and the energy of those you love to restore, restock and replenish your inner resources. To learn to interpret the signal of loneliness correctly. To take responsibility for your own care and resources and to not abdicate your own power to take care of yourself.

Mastery:

The ability to retreat as a way of replenishing your inner and outer resources and to bring your renewed Self back into community when you are ready so that you have more to give.

Unbalanced Expression:

Martyrdom. Loneliness and blaming that causes you to compromise what you need and try to prove your value by overdoing and over-giving.

Resiliency Keys:

Self-Worth: *What needs to be healed, released, aligned and brought to my awareness in order for me to fully acknowledge my value?*

Vitality: *What needs to be healed, released, aligned and brought to my awareness for me to heal from this burnout?*

Empowerment: *What needs to be healed, released, aligned and brought to my awareness for me to feel powerful in this situation?*

Affirmation:

I am a powerful resource for my community. The energy that I hold impacts others deeply and brings them to deeper states of alignment and sustainability. I take care of my body, mind and soul because I know that the more that I am and the more that I have, the more I can give to others. I take care of myself first because I know that good things flow from me. I am valuable and powerful and I claim and defend the true story of Who I Truly Am.

Further Contemplations:

1. *What role does loneliness play in my life? Has loneliness caused me to doubt my value?*

2. *What do I need to do to restore my energy? Am I doing enough to take care of myself?*

3. *What agreements am I making in my relationships that might be causing me to compromise my value? How can I rewrite these agreements?*

4. *Am I abdicating my responsibility for my self-care? Am I living a "martyr" model? What needs to be healed, released, aligned and brought to my awareness for me to take responsibility for cultivating my own sense of value and my self-worth?*

Gate 41: Imagination

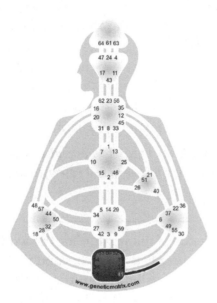

Challenge:

To learn to use your imagination as a source of creative inspiration and manifestation. To experience the world and imagine more abundant possibilities. To stay connected to your creative fire.

Mastery:

The ability to use your creative imagination to generate ideas about new abundant opportunities in the world. To sustain these abundant visions, share them when necessary, and use your imagination to break old patterns and limiting beliefs. To be able to hold the vision of a miracle that transcends expectations.

Unbalanced Expression:

To imagine worst-case scenarios and fixate on them. Denying your creative capacity and abdicating your creative power. Being afraid to share other options because they defy the current expectations or patterns. Being afraid of being judged by others for being a "dreamer".

Resiliency Keys:

Vitality: *What needs to be healed, released, aligned and brought to my awareness for me to heal from this burnout?*

Empowerment: *What needs to be healed, released, aligned and brought to my awareness for me to feel powerful in this situation?*

Affirmation:

I am a creative nexus of inspiration for the world. My ideas and imaginings inspire people to think beyond their limitations. My ideas stimulate new possibilities in the world. I am a powerful creator and my creative thoughts, ideas and inspirations set the stage for miracles and possibilities that will change the story of humanity.

Further Contemplations:

1. *Do I own my creative power? How can I deepen my self-honoring of my creative power?*

2. *What do I do to express my creative abilities?*

3. *What do I do to hold on to my dreams and visions? Am I sustaining them or do I give up? What can I do to deepen my sustainability?*

4. *Do I allow myself to dream of good things? Do I believe in miracles? How can I deepen my faith in the goodness of the world?*

Gate 42: Conclusion

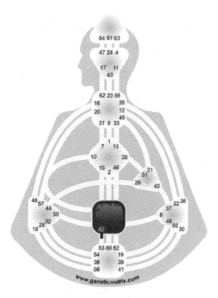

Challenge:

To learn to bring things to completion. To allow yourself to be led to where you need to be to finish things. To value your ability to know how to finish and to learn to give up your need to try to start everything. To finish things in order to create space for something new.

Mastery:

The ability to respond to being inserted into opportunities, experiences and events that you have the wisdom to facilitate and complete. To know exactly what needs to be completed in order to create the space for something new.

Unbalanced Expression:

Pressure, confusion and self-judgement for not being able to "get things started". Avoiding or putting off things that need to be completed creating a backlog of projects that can lead to paralysis and overwhelm. Finishing things prematurely due to pressure.

Resiliency Keys:

Decisiveness: *What needs to be healed, released, aligned and brought to my awareness for me to make clear and strong choices?*

Courage: *What needs to be healed, released, aligned and brought to my awareness for me to move forward with courage and faith?*

Vitality: *What needs to be healed, released, aligned and brought to my awareness for me to heal from this burnout?*

Empowerment: *What needs to be healed, released, aligned and brought to my awareness for me to feel powerful in this situation?*

Affirmation:

I am gifted at knowing when and how to finish things. I respond to bringing events, experiences and relationships to conclusion in order to create space for something new and more abundant. I can untangle the cosmic entanglements that keep people stuck in old patterns. My ability to re-align and complete things helps others create space for transformation and expansion.

Further Contemplations:

1. *Do I own and value my natural gift of knowing how to bring things to completion?*

2. *What things in my life do I need to finish in order to make room for something new?*

3. *Am I holding on to old circumstances and patterns because I'm afraid to let them go?*

4. *Do I judge myself for "not starting things"? How can I learn to be gentler with myself?*

Gate 43: Insight

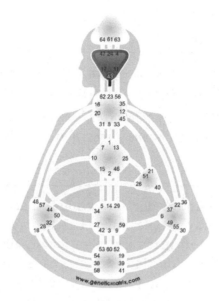

Challenge:

To be comfortable and to trust epiphanies and deep inner knowing without doubting what you know. To trust that when the timing is right, you will know how to share what you know and serve your role as a transformative messenger who has insights that can change the way people think and what they know.

Mastery:

The ability to tap into new knowledge, understandings and insights that expand people's understanding of the world. To align with the right timing and trust that you'll know how to share what you know when you need to share it.

Unbalanced Expression:

Feeling despair or frustration related to having knowledge but struggling to share what you know. Experiencing lightning bolts of knowingness and clarity but feeling overwhelmed by your inability to articulate what you understand. Not waiting for the right time to share what you know and feeling alone with your wisdom.

Resiliency Keys:

Decisiveness: *What needs to be healed, released, aligned and brought to my awareness for me to make clear and strong choices?*

Self-Trust: *What needs to be healed, released, aligned and brought to my awareness in order for me to trust myself and my inner knowing?*

Affirmation:

I am a vessel of knowledge and wisdom that has the ability to transform the way people think. I share my knowledge with others when they are ready and vibrationally aligned with what I have to share. When the time is right, I have the right words and the right insights to help others expand their thinking, re-calibrate their mindset and discover the elegant solutions to the challenges facing Humanity.

Further Contemplations:

1. *Do I trust in Divine Timing?*

2. *Do I trust myself and my own Inner Knowing? What can I do to deepen my connection with my Source of Knowing?*

3. *What needs to be healed, released, aligned or brought to my awareness for me to trust my own Inner Knowing?*

Gate 44: Truth

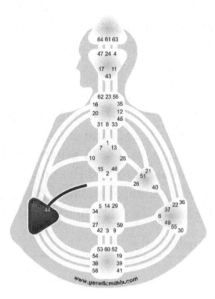

Challenge:

To not get stuck in past patterns. To cultivate the courage to go forward without being stuck in the fear of the past. To learn how to transform pain into power and to have the courage to express your authentic self without compromise or settling.

Mastery:

The ability to see patterns that have created pain. To bring awareness to help yourself and others break old patterns and transform pain into an increased sense of value and alignment with purpose.

Unbalanced Expression:

Fear and paralysis that the patterns of the past are insurmountable and doomed to repeat themselves.

Resiliency Keys:

Self-Trust: *What needs to be healed, released, aligned and brought to my awareness in order for me to trust myself and my inner knowing?*

Courage: *What needs to be healed, released, aligned and brought to my awareness for me to move forward with courage and faith?*

Affirmation:

I am powerfully intuitive and can sense the patterns that keep others stuck in limiting beliefs and constricted action. Through my insights and awareness, I help others break free from past limiting patterns and learn to find the power in their pain, find the blessings in their challenges and help them align more deeply with an authentic awareness of their True Value and Purpose.

Further Contemplations:

1. *What patterns from the past are holding me back from moving forward with courage?*

2. *Do I see how my experiences from the past have helped me learn more about Who I Truly Am? What have I learned about my value and my power?*

3. *What needs to be healed, released, aligned and brought to my awareness for me to fully activate my power?*

4. *What needs to be healed, released, aligned and brought to my awareness for me to step boldly into my aligned and authentic path?*

Gate 45: Distribution

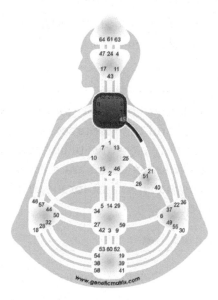

Challenge:

To share and use your resources for the greater good of the whole. To learn to manage resources judiciously so that they benefit the most amount of people. To teach as a pathway of sharing.

Mastery:

The ability to understand that knowledge and material resources are powerful, and to know how to use both as a path of service that sustains others and helps others grow their own abundant foundation.

Unbalanced Expression:

Diva energy. Selfish leadership that is rooted in lack and showing off. Holding back. Overcompensating for a lack of self-worth with narcissism. Fear of not being seen as a leader and reacting by being controlling or bombastic.

Resiliency Keys:

Authenticity: *What needs to be healed, released, aligned and brought to my awareness for me to fully express my Authentic Identity?*

Vitality: *What needs to be healed, released, aligned and brought to my awareness for me to heal from this burnout?*

Affirmation:

I am a teacher and a leader. I use my resources, my knowledge and my experience to expand the resources, knowledge and experiences of others. I use my blessings of abundance to increase the blessings of others. I know that I am a vehicle of wisdom and knowledge. I sense when it's right for me to share who I am and what I know with others.

Further Contemplations:

1. *Do I like to share? What do I have to give the world?*

2. *How do I own my right leadership? Am I comfortable as a leader? Do I shrink from leadership? Do I overcompensate by pushing too hard with my leadership?*

3. *Do I trust that when the right people are ready I will be pressed into action as a leader and a teacher? What do I need to heal, release, align or bring to my awareness to trust my leadership energy more?*

4. *What do I need to heal, release, align or bring to my awareness to trust my leadership energy more?*

Gate 46: Embodiment

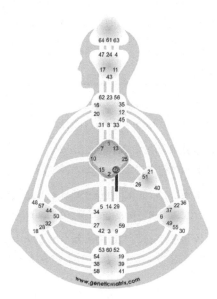

Challenge:

To learn to love your body. To learn to fully be in your body. To learn to love the sensual nature of your physical form and to move it with love and awareness.

Mastery:

To recognize that the body is the vehicle for the soul and to love the body as a vital element of the soul's expression in life. To nurture, be grounded in and fully care for the body. To savor the physicality of the human experience. To explore how to fully embody the spirit in your body and to be committed and devoted to seeing how much life force you can embody into your physical form.

Unbalanced Expression:

To disconnect from the body. To hate the body. To avoid nurturing or taking care of the body. To avoid the commitments and consistency necessary to fully embody life force. To hide or disfigure the body.

Resiliency Keys:

Lovability: *What needs to be healed, released, aligned and brought to my awareness for me to love myself better?*

Decisiveness: *What needs to be healed, released, aligned and brought to my awareness for me to make clear and strong choices?*

Courage: *What needs to be healed, released, aligned and brought to my awareness for me to move forward with courage and faith?*

Authenticity: *What needs to be healed, released, aligned and brought to my awareness for me to fully express my Authentic Identity?*

Affirmation:

My body is the vehicle for my soul. My ability to fully express who I am – and my life and soul purpose – is deeply rooted in my body's ability to carry my soul. I love, nurture and commit to my body. I appreciate all of its miraculous abilities and form. Every day I love my body more.

Further Contemplations:

1. *Do I love my body? What can I do to deepen my love for my body?*

2. *What parts of my body do I love and appreciate? Make a list of every part of my body that I love.*

3. *What do I need to do to amplify the life force I am experiencing in my body?*

4. *What kinds of devotion and commitment do I experience that help me harness greater amounts of life force in my body? How can I deepen my commitment and devotion to my body?*

Gate 47: Mindset

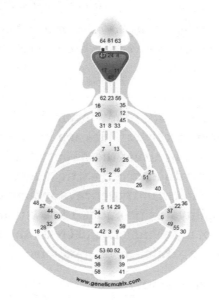

Challenge:

To master a mindset of openness and possibility. To not let inspiration die because you don't know "how" to fulfill it.

Mastery:

To engage in hopeful, inspired thoughts no matter what is going on around you. To use inspiration as a catalyst for calibrating emotional frequency and the Heart.

Unbalanced Expression:

To quit or give up an inspiration because you can't "figure out" how to make it happen. To feel defeated and broken because you think you have ideas that you can't manifest.

Resiliency Keys:

Self-Trust: *What needs to be healed, released, aligned and brought to my awareness in order for me to trust myself and my inner knowing?*

Decisiveness: *What needs to be healed, released, aligned and brought to my awareness for me to make clear and strong choices?*

Affirmation:

My mindset is the source of my inspired actions and attitude. I know that when I receive an idea and inspiration, it is my job to nurture the idea by using the power of my imagination to increase the potential and emotional frequency of the idea. I consistently keep my inner and outer environment aligned with the energy of possibility and potential. I know that it is my job to create by virtue of my alignment and I relax knowing that it's the job of the Universe to fulfill my inspirations.

Further Contemplations:

1. *What thoughts do I have when I receive an idea or inspiration? Am I hopeful or despairing? How does it feel to let go of figuring out "how" I'm going to make my idea a reality?*

2. *What do I do to regulate my mindset? What practices do I need to cultivate to increase the power of my thoughts?*

Gate 48: Wisdom

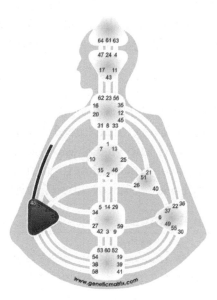

Challenge:

To allow yourself to trust that you'll know what you need to know when you need to know it. To not let the fear of not knowing stop you from creating. To not let "not knowing" hold you back.

Mastery:

The wisdom to explore and learn the depth of knowledge necessary to create a strong foundation for action and mastery. The self-trust to have faith in your ability to know how to know, and to trust your connection to Source as the true source of your knowledge.

Unbalanced Expression:

Paralysis in inadequacy. To be afraid to try something new or to go beyond your comfort zone because you think you don't know or that you're not ready.

Resiliency Keys:

Self-Trust: *What needs to be healed, released, aligned and brought to my awareness in order for me to trust myself and my inner knowing?*

Courage: *What needs to be healed, released, aligned and brought to my awareness for me to move forward with courage and faith?*

Affirmation:

I am a depth of wisdom and knowledge. My studies and experiences have taught me everything I need to know. I push beyond the limits of my earthly knowledge and take great leaps of faith as a function of my deep connection to Source, knowing that I'll always know what I need to know when I need to know it.

Further Contemplations:

1. *Do I trust my own knowing? What needs to be healed, released, aligned and brought to my awareness for me to deepen my self-trust?*

2. *What practice do I have that keeps me connected to the wisdom of Source? How can I deepen my connection to Source?*

Gate 49: The Catalyst

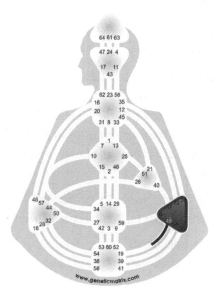

Challenge:

To not quit prematurely. To hold on for longer than is healthy and to settle or compromise your value in situations, relationships and with agreements that aren't worthy of you.

Mastery:

The ability to sense when it's time to hold to a value that supports your value. The ability to inspire others to make expansive changes that embrace higher principles and a deeper alignment with peace and sustainability. The willingness to align with a higher value.

Unbalanced Expression:

Quitting too soon as a way of avoiding intimacy. Compromising on your value and upholding agreements that no longer serve you. Creating drama and fighting for outdated values that no longer serve the higher good.

Resiliency Keys:

Courage: *What needs to be healed, released, aligned and brought to my awareness for me to move forward with courage and faith?*

Emotional Wisdom: *What needs to be healed, released, aligned and brought to my awareness in order for me to be a powerful, deliberate Creator? What needs to be healed, released, aligned and brought to my awareness for me to trust my emotional energy? What needs to be healed, released, aligned and brought to my awareness for me to ask for what I want and need?*

Empowerment: *What needs to be healed, released, aligned and brought to my awareness for me to feel powerful in this situation?*

Decisiveness: *What needs to be healed, released, aligned and brought to my awareness for me to make clear and strong choices?*

Affirmation:

I am a cosmic revolutionary. I am aligned with higher principles that support the evolution of humanity. I stand for peace, equity and sustainability. I align with these principles and I stand my ground. I do the work to create the intimacy necessary to share my values with others. I value myself and my work enough to only align with relationships that support my vital role.

Further Contemplations:

1. *Am I holding on too long? Is there a circumstance and condition that I am allowing because I am afraid of the emotional energy associated with change?*

2. *Do I have a habit of quitting too soon? Do I fail to do the work associated with creating genuine intimacy?*

3. *What do I need to let go of right now to create room for me to align with higher principles?*

Gate 50: Nurturing

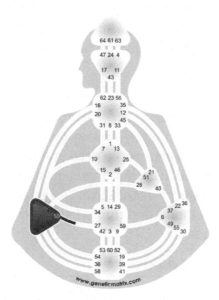

Challenge:

To transcend guilt and unhealthy obligation and do what you need to do to take care of yourself in order to better serve others. To hold to rigid principles to judge others.

Mastery:

The ability to nurture yourself so that you have more to give others. The intuition to know what others need to bring them into greater alignment with Love. To teach and share what you have to increase the wellbeing of others.

Unbalanced Expression:

To over-care. To let guilt stop you from sustaining yourself. To hold to rigid principles and to struggle to allow others the consequences of their choices.

Resiliency Keys:

Self-Trust: *What needs to be healed, released, aligned and brought to my awareness in order for me to trust myself and my inner knowing?*

Courage: *What needs to be healed, released, aligned and brought to my awareness for me to move forward with courage and faith?*

Affirmation:

My presence brings Love into the room. I nurture and love others. I take care of myself first in order to be better able to serve Love. I intuit what people need and I facilitate for them a state of self-love and self-empowerment by helping them align more deeply with the power of Love. I let go and I allow others to learn from what I model and teach. I am a deep well of love that sustains the planet.

Further Contemplations:

1. *How do I feel about taking care of myself first? How do I sustain my nurturing energy?*

2. *What role does guilt play in driving and/or motivating you? What would you choose if your could remove the guilt?*

3. *Do you have non-negotiable values? What are they? How do you handle people who share different values from you?*

Gate 51: Initiation

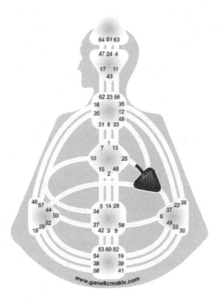

www.geneticmatrix.com

Challenge:

To not let the unexpected cause you to lose your faith. To not let a pattern of unexpected events cause you to lose your connection with your purpose and Source. To learn to use the power of your own story of initiation to initiate others into fulfilling their right place in the Cosmic Plan.

Mastery:

The ability to consciously use cycles of disruption and unexpected twists and turns of faith as catalysts that deepen your connection to Source and to your Life and Soul Purpose.

Unbalanced Expression:

To let the shock of disruption cause you to lose connection with your true purpose and with Source. To become bitter or angry with God. To try to control life and deplete yourself from the energy necessary to hold yourself back.

Resiliency Keys:

Self-Worth: *What needs to be healed, released, aligned and brought to my awareness in order for me to fully acknowledge my value?*

Vitality: *What needs to be healed, released, aligned and brought to my awareness for me to heal from this burnout?*

Empowerment: *What needs to be healed, released, aligned and brought to my awareness for me to feel powerful in this situation?*

Affirmation:

I navigate change and transformation with Grace. I know that when my life takes a twist or a turn, it is my soul calling me out to serve at a higher level. I use disruption as a catalyst for my own growth and expansion. I am a teacher and an initiator. I use my ability to transform pain into growth and power to help others navigate through crisis and emerge on the other side of crisis empowered and aligned.

Further Contemplations:

1. *What has shock and the unexpected taught me in my life?*

2. *How can I deepen my connection to Source?*

3. *How can my experiences of initiation be shared with others? What am I here to "wake people up" to?*

Gate 52: Perspective

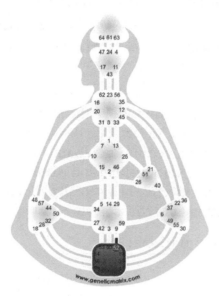

www.geneticmatrix.com

Challenge:

To learn to stay focused even when you're overwhelmed by a bigger perspective. To see the "big picture" and to not let the massive nature of what you know confuse you and cause you to struggle with where to put your energy and attention.

Mastery:

The ability to see the bigger perspective and purpose of what is going on around you and to know exactly where to focus your energy and attention to facilitate the unfolding of what's next.

Unbalanced Expression:

Attention deficit. To let overwhelm paralyze you and cause you to fail to act. To put your energy and attention in the wrong place and to spend your energy focused on something that bears no fruit.

Resiliency Keys:

Vitality: *What needs to be healed, released, aligned and brought to my awareness for me to heal from this burnout?*

Empowerment: *What needs to be healed, released, aligned and brought to my awareness for me to feel powerful in this situation?*

Affirmation:

I am like the eagle soaring above the land. I see the entirety of what needs to happen to facilitate the evolution of the world. I use my perspective to see my unique and irreplaceable role in the Cosmic Plan. I see relationships and patterns that others don't always see. My perspective helps us all to build a peaceful world more effectively and in a consciously directed way.

Further Contemplations:

1. *What do I do to maintain and sustain my focus? Is there anything in my environment or my life that I need to move out of the way in order for me to deepen my focus?*

2. *How do I manage feeling overwhelmed? What things am I avoiding because I feel overwhelmed by them? What is one bold action I can take to begin clearing the path for action?*

3. *How does my feeling of being overwhelmed affect my self-worth? How can I love myself more deeply in spite of feeling overwhelmed?*

Gate 53: Starting

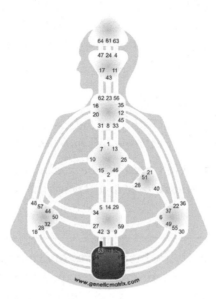

Challenge:

To respond (in alignment with your energy blueprint) to opportunities to get things started. To initiate the process of preparing or "setting the stage" for the manifestation of a dream before it becomes a reality. To learn to trust in the timing of the Universe and not take charge and try to implement your own ideas while working against Divine Timing. To not burn out trying to complete things. To find peace as a "starter", not a "finisher".

Mastery:

The ability to sit with inspiration and be attuned to what the Inspiration wants and needs. To launch the initiation sequence for an idea and initiate it – and then let the idea follow its right course with trust in the flow.

Unbalanced Expression:

Reacting to the pressure to get an idea started. To feel like a failure because everything you start against right timing fails. To be afraid to start anything because of the trauma of your past "failures". Starting everything and never reaping the rewards of what you start.

Resiliency Keys:

Vitality: *What needs to be healed, released, aligned and brought to my awareness for me to heal from this burnout?*

Empowerment: *What needs to be healed, released, aligned and brought to my awareness for me to feel powerful in this situation?*

Affirmation:

I am a servant to Divine Inspiration. My thoughts, inspirations and ideas set the stage for creative expansion and the potential for evolution. I take action on the ideas that present themselves to me in an aligned way. I honor all other ideas, knowing that my gift is in the spark of energy that gets things rolling when the timing is right. While I wait for right timing, I guard my energy and charge my battery so that I am sustainable when the time is right for action.

Further Contemplations:

1. *How do I feel about myself when I have an idea and I can't get it initiated?*

2. *How do I feel when someone takes my initial idea and builds on it? Do I value what I started?*

3. *What identities and attachments do I have to being the one who starts and finishes something?*

4. *Do I judge myself for not finishing something? How can I be more gentle with myself?*

5. *Do I trust Divine Timing? How can I deepen my trust in right timing?*

Gate 54: Divine Inspiration

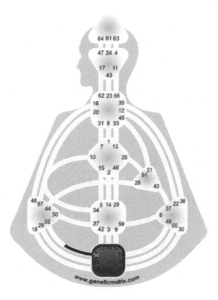

Challenge:

To learn to be a conduit for Divine Inspiration. To be patient and to wait for alignment and right timing before taking action. To be at peace with stewardship for ideas, and to learn to trust the divine trajectory of an inspiration.

Mastery:

The ability to cultivate a deep relationship with the Divine Muse. To nurture the inspirational fruits of the muse, and to serve as a steward for an inspiration by aligning the idea energetically and preparing the way by laying foundational action and building.

Unbalanced Expression:

To react to the pressure that you have to fulfill an inspiration and to use force to push the inspiration into form – even though it might not be your idea/dream to manifest or the right time to bring it forth.

Resiliency Keys:

Vitality: *What needs to be healed, released, aligned and brought to my awareness for me to heal from this burnout?*

Empowerment: *What needs to be healed, released, aligned and brought to my awareness for me to feel powerful in this situation?*

Affirmation:

I am a Divine Conduit for inspiration. Through me, new ideas about creating sustainability and peace on the planet are born. I tend to my inspirations, give them love and energy and prepare the way for their manifestations in the material world.

Further Contemplations:

1. *What do I do to get inspired? How do I interface with my creative muse?*

2. *Is there anything I need to do or prepare in order to be ready for the next step in the manifestation of my dream or inspiration?*

Gate 55: Faith

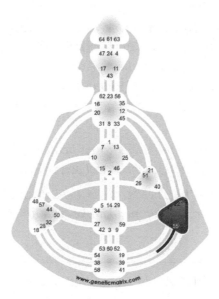

Challenge:

To learn to trust Source. To know that you are fully supported. To master the art of emotional alignment as your most creative power.

Mastery:

The ability to hold the emotional frequency of energy and the vision for a creation. To trust in sufficiency so deeply that you're able to create without limitation.

Unbalanced Expression:

Indecisiveness. Fear and lack. Hoarding, keeping from others, fighting to take more than your share. Not trusting Source and drawing on will to create.

Resiliency Keys:

Courage: *What needs to be healed, released, aligned and brought to my awareness for me to move forward with courage and faith?*

Emotional Wisdom: *What needs to be healed, released, aligned and brought to my awareness in order for me to be a powerful, deliberate Creator? What needs to be healed, released, aligned and brought to my awareness for me to trust my emotional energy? What needs to be healed, released, aligned and brought to my awareness for me to ask for what I want and need?*

Empowerment: *What needs to be healed, released, aligned and brought to my awareness for me to feel powerful in this situation?*

Decisiveness: *What needs to be healed, released, aligned and brought to my awareness for me to make clear and strong choices?*

Affirmation:

I am perfectly and divinely supported. I know that all my needs and desires are being fulfilled. My trust in my support allows me to create beyond the limitation of what others think is possible and my faith shows them the way. I use my emotional energy as the source of my creative power. My frequency of faith lifts others up and opens up a greater world of potential and possibility.

Further Contemplations:

1. *Do I trust that I am fully supported? What do I need to do to deepen that trust?*

2. *How can I align myself with abundant emotional energy? What practices or shifts do I need to make in my life to live and create in a more aligned way?*

3. *Do I surround myself with beauty? How can I deepen my experience of beauty in my life?*

4. *What do I have faith in now? What old gods of limitation do I need to stop worshipping?*

5. *Go on a miracle hunt. Take stock of everything good that has happened in my life. How much "magic" have I been blessed with?*

Gate 56: Expansion

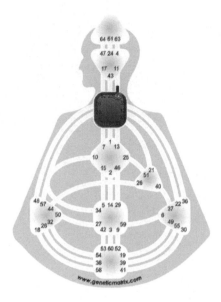

Challenge:

To learn to share stories and inspirations with the right people at the right time. To learn to tell stories of expansion, not depletion and contraction.

Mastery:

The ability to share stories and inspirations that stimulate expansive and possibility-oriented thinking in others for the sake of stimulating powerful emotional energy that creates evolution and growth.

Unbalanced Expression:

To get lost or stuck in stories and narratives that are limiting. To tell stories that contract and deplete the energy of others.

Resiliency Keys:

Authenticity: *What needs to be healed, released, aligned and brought to my awareness for me to fully express my Authentic Identity?*

Vitality: *What needs to be healed, released, aligned and brought to my awareness for me to heal from this burnout?*

Affirmation:

I am a Divine Storyteller. The stories of possibility that I share have the power to inspire others to grow and expand. I use my words as a template for possibility and expansion for the world. I inspire the world with my words.

Further Contemplations:

1. *What stories do I share repeatedly with others? Do they lift people up or cause them to contract?*

2. *What stories do I tell about myself and my voice that cause me to either expand or contract?*

3. *What am I here to inspire others to do or be?*

Gate 57: Instinct

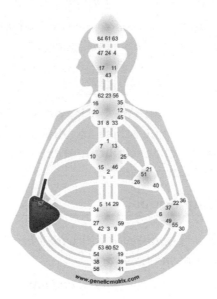

Challenge:

To learn to trust your own insights and "gut". To learn to tell the difference between an instinctive response versus a fear of the future. To master your connection to your sense of "right" timing.

Mastery:

The ability to sense when it is the right time to act. To intuitively know what needs to be made ready to be prepared for the future and to follow through on it.

Unbalanced Expression:

To be so afraid of the future that you are paralyzed. To not trust yourself and your own instinct. To know what needs to be done to prepare for the future and to fail to act on it.

Resiliency Keys:

Self-Trust: *What needs to be healed, released, aligned and brought to my awareness in order for me to trust myself and my inner knowing?*

Courage: *What needs to be healed, released, aligned and brought to my awareness for me to move forward with courage and faith?*

Affirmation:

My Inner Wisdom is deeply connected to the pulse of Divine Timing. I listen to my Inner Wisdom and follow my instinct. I know when and how to prepare the way to prepare for the future. I take guided action and I trust myself and Source.

Further Contemplations:

1. *Do I trust my intuition? What does my intuition feel like to me?*

2. *Sometimes doing a retrospective analysis of my intuition/instinct makes it more clear how my intuitive signal works. What experiences in the past have I had that I "knew" I should or shouldn't do? How have I experienced my intuition in the past?*

3. *When I think about moving forward in my life, do I feel afraid? What am I afraid of? What can I do to mitigate the fear?*

4. *What impulses am I experiencing that are telling me to prepare for what's next in my life? Am I acting on my impulses? Why or why not?*

Gate 58: The Joy of Mastery

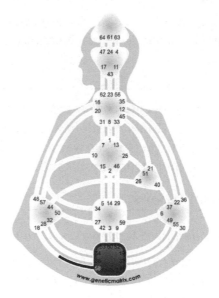

Challenge:

To follow the drive to create the fulfillment of your potential. To learn to craft a talent and make it masterful through joyful learning and repetition. To learn to embrace joy as a vital force of creative power without guilt or denial.

Mastery:

To harness the joy of mastery and refine your practice until you reach fulfillment of your potential. To live in the flow of Joy.

Unbalanced Expression:

To deny joy. To avoid the practice of mastery. To feel guilty or ashamed to do what you love. To disbelieve in joy.

Resiliency Keys:

Vitality: *What needs to be healed, released, aligned and brought to my awareness for me to heal from this burnout?*

Empowerment: *What needs to be healed, released, aligned and brought to my awareness for me to feel powerful in this situation?*

Affirmation:

I am a masterful curator of my own talent. I use my joy to drive me to master the fun expression of all that I am. I practice as my path to mastery. I know that from repetition and consistency comes a more masterful expression of my talent. I embrace learning and growing and I commit to the full expression of my joy.

Further Contemplations:

1. *What brings me the greatest joy? How can I deepen my practice of joy?*

2. *How can I create more joy in my life?*

3. *What keeps me from fulfilling my potential and my talent? What am I afraid of?*

Gate 59: Sustainability

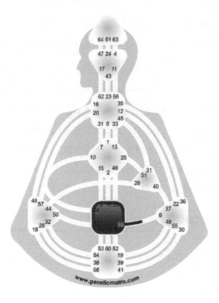

Challenge:

To learn to make abundant choices that sustain you and, at the same time, others. To collaborate and initiate others into sustainable relationships from a place of sufficiency. To learn to share what you have in a sustainable way.

Mastery:

To trust in sufficiency and to know that when you create abundance there is great fulfillment in sharing. To craft partnerships and relationships that sustain you and the foundation of your lives.

Unbalanced Expression:

To feel like you have to fight or struggle to survive. To feel the need to penetrate others and force your "rightness" on them. To let fear of lack cause you to craft relationships and agreements that are unsustainable.

Resiliency Keys:

Decisiveness: *What needs to be healed, released, aligned and brought to my awareness for me to make clear and strong choices?*

Courage: *What needs to be healed, released, aligned and brought to my awareness for me to move forward with courage and faith?*

Vitality: *What needs to be healed, released, aligned and brought to my awareness for me to heal from this burnout?*

Empowerment: *What needs to be healed, released, aligned and brought to my awareness for me to feel powerful in this situation?*

Affirmation:

The energy that I carry has the power to create sufficiency and sustainability for all. I craft valuable alliances and agreements that support me in expanding abundance for everyone. I hold to higher principles and values that are rooted in my trust in sufficiency and the all-providing Source. Through my work and alignments, my blessings serve to increase the blessings of myself and others.

Further Contemplations:

1. *Do I trust in my own abundance?*

2. *How do I feel about sharing what I have with others?*

3. *Am I creating relationship and partnership agreements that honor my work?*

4. *Do I have relationships and agreements that are draining me? What needs to change?*

5. *How do I feel about being "right"? Am I open to other ways of thinking or being? Do I believe in creating agreements and alignments with people who have different values and perspectives?*

Gate 60: Conservation

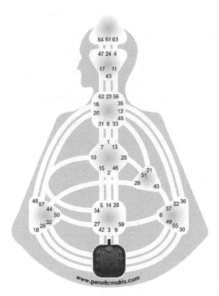

Challenge:

To not let the fear of loss overwhelm your resourcefulness. To learn to find what is working and focus on it instead of looking at the loss and disruption.

Mastery:

The ability to find the blessings in transformation. Optimism. To know how to focus on what is working instead of what's not.

Unbalanced Expression:

To hold on and not allow for growth. To fight for the old and rebuke change. To let the overwhelm of change and disruption create paralysis and resistance.

Resiliency Keys:

Vitality: *What needs to be healed, released, aligned and brought to my awareness in order for me to trust myself and my inner knowing?*

Empowerment: *What needs to be healed, released, aligned and brought to my awareness for me to move forward with courage and faith?*

Affirmation:

I am grateful for all the transformation and change in my life. I know that disruption is the catalyst for my growth. I am able to find the blessings of the past and incorporate them in my innovative vision for the future. I am optimistic about the future and I transform the world by growing what works.

Further Contemplations:

1. *What change am I resisting? What am I afraid of?*
2. *What are the things in my life that are working that I need to focus on?*
3. *Is my fear of loss holding me back?*

Gate 61: Wonder

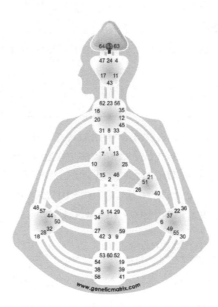

Challenge:

To not get lost in trying to answer or figure out why? To maintain a state of wonder and awe. To not let the pressure of trying to "know" keep you from being present.

Mastery:

The ability to see purpose in a bigger perspective that transcends the smaller details of an experience or event. The ability to stay in a state of innocence and delusional confidence as a way of sustaining powerful creativity.

Unbalanced Expression:

Allowing the pressure to know "why" to create bitterness or victimhood that is often perpetuated in a rationalized pattern.

Resiliency Keys:

Decisiveness: *What needs to be healed, released, aligned and brought to my awareness for me to make clear and strong choices?*

Self-trust: *What needs to be healed, released, aligned and brought to my awareness in order for me to trust myself and my inner knowing?*

Affirmation:

I have a direct connection to a cosmic perspective that gives me an expanded view of the meaning of the events in my life and the lives of others. I see the wonder and innocence of life and stay present in a constant state of awe. I am innocent and pure in my understanding of the world, and my innocence is the source of my creative alignment.

Further Contemplations:

1. *What do I do to maintain my sense of wonder? How can I deepen my awe of the magnificence of the Universe?*

2. *What old thoughts, patterns and beliefs do I need to release in order to align with my knowingness and to trust my "delusional confidence" as a powerful creative state.*

3. *What greater perspectives on the events of my life can I see? What are the greatest lessons I've learned from my pain? How do I use these lessons to expand my self-expression?*

Gate 62: Preparation

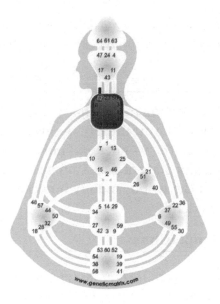

Challenge:

To trust that you'll be prepared for the next step. To not let worry and over-preparation detract you from being present to the moment. To let the fear of not being ready keep you trapped.

Mastery:

The ability to be attuned to what is necessary to be prepared, and to trust that your alignment will inform you of everything that you need. Relaxing and knowing that you'll know what you need to know when you need to know it.

Unbalanced Expression:

Fear and worry. Over-preparation. Allowing the plan to override the "flow"

Resiliency Keys:

Authenticity: *What needs to be healed, released, aligned and brought to my awareness for me to fully express my Authentic Identity?*

Vitality: *What needs to be healed, released, aligned and brought to my awareness for me to heal from this burnout?*

Affirmation:

I create the foundation for the practice of mastery by engineering the plan of action that creates growth. I am in the flow of my understanding and I use my knowledge and experience to be prepared for the evolution of what's next. I am ready and I am prepared. I trust my own preparation and allow myself to be in the flow of what's next, knowing that I'll know what I need to know when I need to know it.

Further Contemplations:

1. *Do I worry? What do I do to manage my worry?*

2. *What can I do to trust that I know what I need to know? What proof do I have that I am in the flow of preparation?*

3. *Is there anything in my life right now that I need to plan for? Am I over- planning? Does my need for contingency plans keep me stuck?*

Gate 63: Curiosity

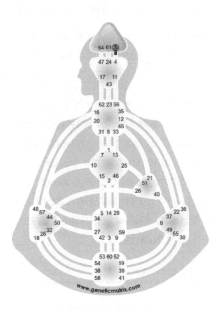

Challenge:

To not let self-doubt and suspicion cause you to stop being curious.

Mastery:

The ability to use questioning and curiosity as a way of stimulating dreams of new possibilities and potentials. Thoughts that inspire the question of what needs to happen to make an idea a reality.

Unbalanced Expression:

Doubt (especially self-doubt) that leads to suspicion and the struggle for certainty. The unwillingness to question an old idea. The loss of curiosity.

Resiliency Keys:

Decisiveness: *What needs to be healed, released, aligned and brought to my awareness for me to make clear and strong choices?*

Self-trust: *What needs to be healed, released, aligned and brought to my awareness in order for me to trust myself and my inner knowing?*

Affirmation:

My curiosity makes me a conduit of possibility thinking. I ask questions that stimulate imaginations. I allow the questions of my mind to seed dreams that stimulate my imagination and the imagination of others. I share my questions as an opening to the fulfillment of potential in the world.

Further Contemplations:

1. *Am I curious about life? Do I regularly allow myself to be curious about what else is possible in the world? In my life?*

2. *Do I doubt myself and my ideas?*

3. *What needs to happen for me to unlock my need to be right about an idea and to allow myself to dream of possibilities again?*

Gate 64: Divine Transference

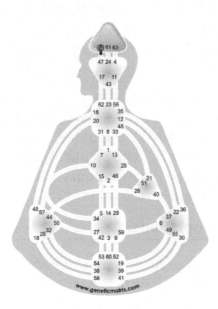

Challenge:

To not let the power of your big ideas overwhelm you and shut down your dreaming and creating. To get lost in the pressure of answering the question "how"?

Mastery:

The ability to receive a "big idea" and to serve the idea by giving it your imagination and dreaming. To trust that you'll know how to implement the idea if it is yours to make manifest. To hold the energy of an idea for the world.

Unbalanced Expression:

To feel pressure to try to "manifest" a big idea. To feel despairing or inadequate or ungrounded if you don't know how to make an idea a reality. To feel deep mental pressure to "figure" out an idea. To give up dreaming.

Resiliency Keys:

Decisiveness: *What needs to be healed, released, aligned and brought to my awareness for me to make clear and strong choices?*

Self-trust: *What needs to be healed, released, aligned and brought to my awareness in order for me to trust myself and my inner knowing?*

Affirmation:

I am a conduit for expansive thinking. My inspirations and ideas create the seeds of possibility in my mind and in the mind of others. I honor the dreams that pass through my mind and allow my big ideas to stimulate my imagination and the imagination of others. I trust the Universe to reveal the details of my dreams when the time is right. I use the power of my dreams to stimulate a world of possibility and expansion.

Further Contemplations:

1. *What do I do to take care of my Big Ideas?*
2. *How do I feel about having "dreams" but not always the solutions?*
3. *How can I stop judging the gift of my dreams?*
4. *Do I trust that the "how" of my ideas will be revealed? How can I deepen this trust?*

 KAREN CURRY PARKER is an expert in Quantum Human Design and developed a system to help explore the relationship between Quantum Physics and Human Design. She's the creator of *Quantum Conversations*, a successful podcast with over 90,000 downloads in less than twelve months, and two systems of Human Design: Quantum Human DesignTM and the Quantum Alignment SystemTM. Multiple news outlets, radio shows, and tele-summits have featured her work on their programs.

Karen is also the author of numerous bestselling books all designed to help you create the life you were destined to live and find and embrace the purpose of your existence.

Karen is available for private consultations, keynote talks, and to conduct in-house seminars and workshops.

You can reach her at Karen@quantumalignmentsystem.com.

Made in the USA
Las Vegas, NV
08 May 2023